Continue move down, out of pitch darkness, into rock face from midian. Title. LAP

DISSOLVE

Continue move down, over graffiti and design covered wall, into which a living face is set. Credits begin.

Books by Clive Barker

THE BOOKS OF BLOOD I-VI
THE DAMNATION GAME
WEAVEWORLD
CABAL
THE GREAT AND SECRET SHOW

Films by Clive Barker

HELLRAISER (DIRECTOR)
HELLBOUND – HELLRAISER II (EXECUTIVE PRODUCER)
NIGHTBREED (WRITER/DIRECTOR)

CLIVE BARKER'S
NIGHTBREED

THE MAKING OF THE FILM

Foreword and Screenplay by
CLIVE BARKER

Introduction by
MARK SALISBURY AND
JOHN GILBERT

FONTANA / Collins

The publishers are grateful to the following for
additional illustrative material:
Steve Hardie, Production Designer   Ricky Eyres, Art Director
Julian Parry, Visual Effects Designer
Tom Brown, Draughtsman   Dave Allday, Draughtsman

Photograph on page 239 © Marcia May

First published in Great Britain by Fontana Paperbacks 1990

Printed and bound in Great Britain by
William Collins & Co Ltd, Glasgow

CONTENTS

FOREWORD

M ovies change; and change; and change.

The images that first play on the screen inside your skull as you set pen to paper are subject to constant configuration. First you cast the faces to go with the characters, and costume them, and make them up; then the actors add their own embellishments to the dialogue, and the lighting cameraman has his contribution, and the set dresser his, and so on and so forth. But that's only the beginning. The image, though fixed on celluloid, is still malleable in countless ways. The editor, placing one action beside another, can change the significance of each; can re-order dialogue, making new sense of old ideas. The optical effects men may create paintings that will put cities where there were none before, and just as magically remove them. The labs can make noon into twilight, or vice versa. Then, sound: another world of significance, transforming the way we perceive the picture on the screen; and music, to signal our responses.

What at first may seem the most immutable of media is in fact capable of being transformed at dozens of stages on its way from screenplay to screen.

As both a writer and a director I am involved in the full spectrum of these processes. Inevitably, during the long, long trail from word to premiere, spirits soar and dive, ideas one day seeming god-given and the next rejected as hellish; decisions becoming badges of honour or yokes.

Somewhere half way through this journey I'm setting these words on paper. Maybe the profoundest doubts about this project are past, and I'm finally on safe ground, believing we've made a good movie: but I'm laying no bets. We've still got another two weeks of shooting to do, much of it related to special effects; that material has then to be cut into the picture. Mattes have yet to be painted, cells animated, titles created, music composed . . .

So much still to do. So many decisions still to make, and every one with its consequences. Still it's time – publishing schedules being what they are – for me to write the introduction to the book of the film.

What follows is, I hope, more than a paste-up of script and movie stills. We've included sketches, scribbles, blueprints and polaroids, hoping to offer some hint of the complexity of the process; a testament to the many hands that shape the finished film. I won't waste space here retelling the story. The script laid out on the following pages, albeit subject to considerable change before the film hits the screen, will do that. What I will try to offer is a glimpse of the story *behind* the story. To try and describe how this first chapter of the Breed's epic came into my head, and what narrative trails spread from it.

For me, one of the great attractions of the interlocked and interdependent collection of genres that constitute the *fantastique* – horror fiction, speculative or science fiction, sword and sorcery fiction – is the clarity with which they run from their present manifestations back to mythological and folkloric roots. The ghost story, the prophetic vision, the chronicle of imagined travels, imagined worlds, imagined conditions – all of these are as vital today, and as popular, as they ever were. Their tradition is honourable, and scattered everywhere with masterpieces. Their current interpreters – in prose and celluloid – are, at their best, producing works that dive head-first into the dream pool we all swim around in during our sleeping lives. Twenty-five years of our projected seventy-five will be spent in that pool. It's important that we learn the strokes.

Perhaps the story-form that fascinates me most is that of the lost or wandering tribe. I treated it first in *Weaveworld,* a book about the Seerkind, who still possessed a holy magic in a secular and rationalist world. Now, in *Nightbreed* I'm creating another tribe, but a very different one. The Kind was an essentially benign species. The Breed are not. They're the monstrous flip side of the coin; a collection of transformers, cannibals and freaks. Their story, as set down in *Cabal*, and now re-envisioned in *Nightbreed*, is in a long tradition of night-quests: a visit by members of our species

into the haunted underground to confront buried mysteries. Those mysteries bite. Several of the Breed have an appetite for human meat. Some are more bestial than human; others have a touch of the Devil in them, and are proud of the fact. To set foot in their domain is to risk death at their hands. But it is also a chance to see the lives of Naturals like ourselves from another perspective. The workings of the world seem a little more preposterous through the eyes of monsters. The Breed have been persecuted in the name of loving God; nearly exterminated by people who have envy in their hearts as much as hatred. As Rachel, one of the characters in the film, tells Lori:

'To be able to fly? To be smoke, or a wolf; to know the night, and live in it forever? That's not so bad. You call us monsters. But when you dream, it's of flying, and changing, and living without death.'

That's one of the perspectives that makes the story of the Breed so intriguing to me. The adventure of *Nightbreed* is as much psychic as physical; or rather the two in one. A descent into a darkness that may illuminate.

Another is less conceptual. It's to do with the challenge of making the insolid solid, and here the business of cinema and the business of fantasy offer interesting parallels.

I use the word *business* advisedly, because, however much I may like to pretend otherwise (and I do), the making of motion pictures is as much commerce as art. That may not be true of more modestly scaled pictures, but a fantasy movie like *Nightbreed,* with countless action sequences, elaborate special effects, and a sizeable cast, costs too much of somebody else's money for me to be left to run creatively riot. Producers watch, accountants account; questions are asked hourly: 'How many more shots to finish this sequence?'; 'Do you *really* need three stuntmen?'; 'Can't we do without the tame pig?' Compromises are beaten out and agreed upon. Small furies come and go.

So the problem is: how do I make the dream real? How do I juggle the possibilities, knowing that visions cost hard cash and I can't have all of dreamland? Clawing something valid from the maelstrom has repeatedly come close to defeating me, but working with the *fantastique* toughens the grip. It is perhaps the very nature of both genre and medium that it try and slip away, and it's *certainly* my nature to attempt to pin it down for a little time, and keep its company.

One of the great pleasures of working in the area of dream-film (if that isn't tautological) is the certainty that its true significance lies as much inside the head of the audience after it has seen the picture as with what I actually put on screen. Much has been written about the way the rise and rise of the craft of special effects has changed the dynamic of such films. The creatures that in earlier years might have been kept discreetly in shadow, allowed only the briefest screen-time, are now often centre stage. In *Nightbreed* I've taken full advantage of this facility, seeking to put on screen more than a few tantalizing glimpses of the creatures. We've created a city for them, a religion, a whole way of life. They are as real, as rounded, as the human characters; in some cases perhaps more so. It's my hope that audiences will take these creations to heart as they did (much against my expectations) with the Cenobites in *Hellraiser*, demanding to know more about their origins and powers, happy to embrace them despite the fact that (or perhaps *because*) they are on the side of darkness.

A movie is a two-hour experience, but if an image or a character touches some nerve in the audience, its effect may last a good deal longer. Some sixty years after they were made *King Kong* and *The Bride of Frankenstein* – two of my favourite dark fantasy films, both focused as much on their fantastical stars as on the human – exercise considerable fascination for audiences. Karloff and Kong are recognizable images the world over, despite the fact that the films in which they appeared are technically far inferior to those of today. It would be overweening of me to claim (or even hope) that our Breed will join that elevated league of icons, but I'd like to think we're producing images that will at least remain in the audience's head longer than a few hours.

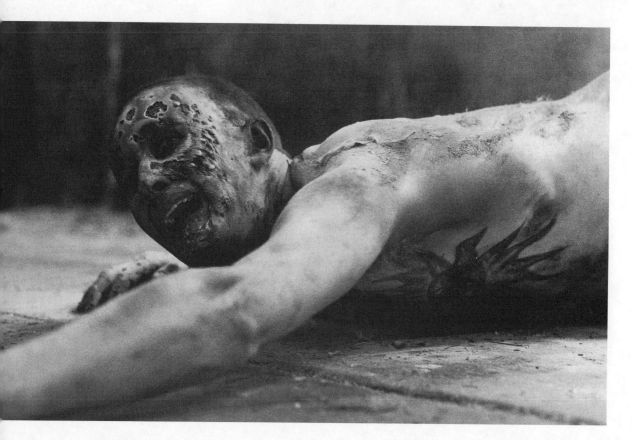

Sooner or later the mask maker, much preoccupied with the art of haunting his audience, becomes haunted himself. How could he not, surrounded day in day out by the faces of his creations? I am, I confess, now so possessed by the Breed that they seem as real to me as the people walking up and down the street outside. I've lived with them like soul-mates, and their story has become a chapter in my own life. If the film communicates even a taste of that reality I'll be well satisfied.

In both the film and the book the head honcho of Midian, Lylesburg, is much preoccupied with the fact that the Breed must remain hidden. *What's below remains below,* he keeps insisting. But fantasy is a kind of archaeology; the digging up of buried images from the psyche; the bringing to light of hidden wonders. The movement of this story is indeed *into* the underground, but then – inevitably – we rise again, with new companions by our side. I hope they haunt you a little.

A HYMN TO THE MONSTROUS

ACKNOWLEDGEMENTS

To Clive Barker for the movie, Murray Close, Stephen Jones, Steve Hardie, Peter Atkins, Bob and Geoff, all at Image Animation, Nicholas Vince, David Cronenberg, Carina, Louise and Stephanie, Gabriella Martinelli, Skipp and Spector, Shaun Hutson, Jim Robinson, Christopher Figg, Richard Marden, Sarah, Craig Sheffer, Anne Bobby, Charlie Haid, Robin Vidgeon, Doug Bradley, Simon Bamford, Oliver Parker and our parents.

And very special thanks to Joanne Osborne, for everything.

'This movie has something for everybody:
mass murders, destruction, monsters!'

Gabriella Martinelli
SUPERVISING PRODUCER

'It's the *Cleopatra* of horror films.'

Steve Jones
UNIT PUBLICIST

The old gods are the new devils, or so the Bible would have us believe. Demons sport horns, vampires sprout fangs and ghouls wear shrouds. Such is the way of the world and it takes a brave man to challenge that view.

Clive Barker is no respecter of convention. Both his books and films reveal a propensity for the outlandish, the subversive and the perverse. His directorial debut, *Hellraiser,* and its sequel *Hellbound* – a film Barker is not satisfied with – continued his avowed intent to smash the boundaries of established genres and provide a bridge between reality and fantasy. Perceptions change, stereotypes are warped, until we no longer know what is homely, good, safe or clean.

Midian represents all those ideals. First glimpsed in his novel, *Cabal,* it is a refuge for the Outsider, the monstrous twists of nature; a community of beasts hidden under the prairies of Canada. It is also an integral part of Clive Barker.

'He's unique,' says *Nightbreed*'s producer Jim Robinson. 'He has the ability to come up with ideas that scare the shit out of you and revolt you.

'I thought if we could have him do with film what he obviously has done in his books then we would be able to turn out some bright, chilling and unique, horror films.'

Barker admits to inexperience on *Hellraiser* but also feels that he is well prepared for the mammoth task of directing this movie. 'I think I know what I want on this picture and maybe I didn't know on *Hellraiser,* simply because it was my first picture. Having said that, the scale of problems on this is massively larger. We're making a small epic of the *fantastique.*'

Casting began in early January 1989 at the same time that the novel *Cabal* was published in the UK. Five months earlier Clive had sat down with Bob Keen and Geoff Portass of special effects company Image Animation and revealed the story of Boone, Lori and the creatures of Midian.

'Clive is a great storyteller,' says special effects supervisor Bob Keen. 'Before he'd written the book he told Geoff and I the story, from notes. We sat for three, four hours and just listened. So, from day one you're dealing with a concept. Even before that script was written, before the book was written, we were dealing with ideas straight from his head. You're never in any doubt of what you're doing.'

Barker was captivated with the idea of having a history of monsters, especially of a conflict between two sets of monsters; in the film's case pitting base humanity against the Breed.

'There are three kinds of monsters in this picture,' explains Barker, 'the Breed; the human monsters, as represented by Eigerman and Ashberry; and the late twentieth-century psycho-on-the-loose, as played by Decker. And that's the three quite distinct and discrete elements. I find that intriguing because I have always loved the creatures of the night and here was the chance to have a compendium.

'We've only got to B so far, but we'll get there,' he promises.

'The idea for *Cabal* had been around for a long time. What happened, however, was the book became bigger and bigger. And then I ended up with a mythology, or at least the beginning of a mythology, which was much larger than I ever thought it was going to be. That's intriguing to me, that's exciting because I have the chance of expanding that on the page and then maybe, if this first picture is successful, expanding it in turn in another picture if I live that long and don't get too exhausted.'

He sent the book to Morgan Creek, a relatively new production company which had been responsible for David Cronenberg's *Dead Ringers*, the brat-pack western *Young Guns*, and the Blake Edwards comedy *Skindeep*. 'They loved it. Joe Roth (*Nightbreed*'s executive producer) who bought the rights went ga-ga. It was great to have that support and enthusiasm for the material.

'Then they gave us the dosh!'

'It's the biggest monster movie ever made.'

Bob Keen
CREATURE DESIGNER

To recreate Midian and its unique race of undead inhabitants on film, Barker required five soundstages at Pinewood Studios in Buckinghamshire, home of the Bond Stage and *Batman*'s Gotham City, and a forty-strong team of special effects experts.

More than two hundred monsters were fleshed out even before the roles of Boone and Lori were cast. Barker was trying to get away from traditional vampires and ghouls. His aim was to make the monsters believable good guys.

'They are scary at first,' says Keen. 'And then become very sympathetic and you begin to see past the grotesqueness of them.

'You're allowed the luxury of getting to know them. Also, since the majority of the leads are monsters, this is a first. The idea was to get away from the horrific images of *Hellraiser,* to look for an art image, and all the concepts grew from that.

'Nothing was planned. Clive wanted to find new ideas, new ways of making people look different. He used to get a couple of people to come in and strip them naked!

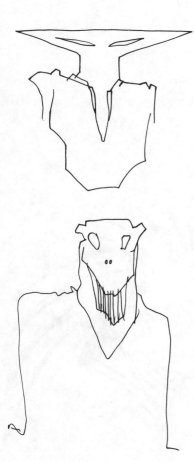

'We knew that the creatures wouldn't all have prosthetics on or be particularly monstrous in form. We came in and wrapped people in string, put bones on their heads, wrapped them in cling film, anything like that to try and experiment with looks rather than with techniques. Once we got those looks the clothing guys came in and made lots of stuff from all the Oxfam shops, making coats out of fifty cardigans or making trousers out of a hundred ties.'

As director, Barker had to deal with the human element in the creature equation. Just how do you get an actor to portray a believable member of the Breed? Fortunately, his experience on *Hellraiser,* where Doug Bradley (Lylesburg) played Pinhead and Nicholas Vince (Kinski) Chatterer, had enabled him to see how the problem could be solved. 'I think one of the things that seldom gets said is that you're asking people to play beings that have no root in that actor's experience.

'Actors normally delve into past experience, emotions such as grief, and try to use that feeling. When you're playing Peloquin or the head Cenobite, there's very little to grasp on to. You have to find another, essentially imaginary, reality, a parallel life. There has to be a greater act of faith between the director and the actor.'

That act of faith also had to be carried across to the human contingent on *Nightbreed* who either become Breed

or have dealings with the creatures. As Barker got to know his cast more intimately he sometimes built aspects of their personalities, histories and interests into the storyline.

Anne-Marie Bobby (Lori) was interested in Channelling, in which the channeller calls upon a spirit guide to aid creative endeavours, while Malcolm Smith left Barker ruing his missed opportunity to use some real-life ancestry for his characterisation. 'I knew about the Channelling,' says Barker, 'although I don't think I was aware how thorough her passion for it was. I also didn't realise that Malcolm Smith's grandfather was a preacher. If I had, I would have done more of the fire and brimstone.

'Filming is a marriage of at least two minds. There's the director/writer and the actor. I hadn't seen how tough and feisty Anne was. I built it in and it worked out of all proportion. I am delighted by the fact that Lori is never the conventional heroine in jeopardy. Nobody fucks around with her.'

Not even Dr Decker.

The movie's two most important creations are Baphomet – Midian's ten-foot high god – and the hideously transformed Boone. In the original novel Baphomet takes the form of a swirling pillar of fire in which the god's dismembered body is enshrined.

For the film, however, Portass had tried out numerous design concepts for Baphomet before Barker called one morning to say he had a solution. That day he produced a full-sized sketch, culled from a dream, transforming the god into a huge living statue whose innards would eventually be filled with fibre-optics. 'Clive wanted it to look more human than monstrous,' explains the special effects designer.

The result, according to Portass, took on a religious aura. 'Its pose in the movie almost resembles a crucifixion. To my mind if you're going to have a god you've got to want to worship him.'

The nature of Baphomet was not fully explained in the first script, but during production Barker inserted an additional scene involving Lylesburg, the patriarch of Midian, which describes the god as an onyx statue destroyed, vandalised and broken down. His hallowed remains are worshipped by the populace of Midian.

The search for an actor to play Baphomet fortunately proved less complicated than the design of the god. As Portass recalls, 'I went through about six black guys to find the one I wanted because only black guys have those certain facial features that needed to be in Baphomet.'

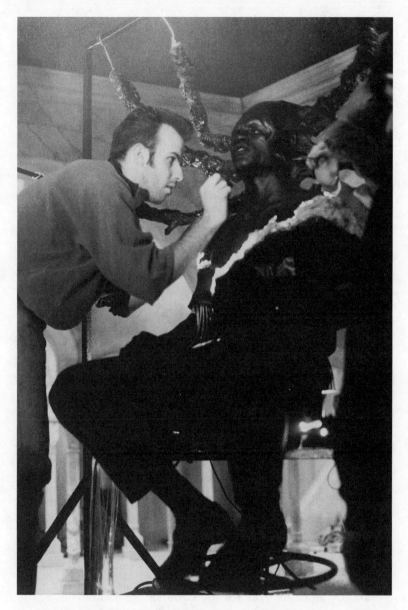

Keen and Portass scoured the photographic files of model agencies to find the god of Clive's dreams. Their eventual choice, Bernard Henry, had no idea what was expected of him when he arrived at Image Animation's Pinewood headquarters for a screen test but, unlike his predecessors, he rose to the occasion.

Portass was instantly impressed by Henry's looks and acting ability. 'The original drawing I've got from Clive looked like Bernard. As soon as I saw him I said, "This is him", even before I'd seen everybody else.'

'Clive's the Bergman of horror.'

Craig Sheffer
ACTOR (BOONE)

Finding the right actor for the pivotal role of Boone proved a near-impossible task with Christopher Lambert and Rutger Hauer reputedly among the many considered, but finally, just six weeks before shooting began, Barker chose American actor Craig Sheffer whose heroic physique was cultivated in the time before an unfortunate accident put paid to a promising professional football career. Sheffer, who had previously been seen in Emilo Estevez's screenwriting debut, *That Was Then, This Is Now*, and John Hughes's *Some Kind of Wonderful*, provided his character with just the right amount of tortured innocence; his unusual good looks a godsend for Barker, who was determined his leading man should not fit the traditional mould.

'Boone is a guy who's had a lot of trouble in the past, he's a schizophrenic manic depressive,' says the taciturn Sheffer of his role. 'I think the problem's been he's been vibed out all his life. He always picked up strange vibes and has never been able to get his mind under control because there's always been some outside force he couldn't quite put his finger on. But he knew he was different.'

Boone is a monster but is also responsive to emotion. 'When Craig came back for the enhancement shoots after the finish of principal photography,' says Barker, 'we worked together to find a thread of delicacy in him. We were looking always for Boone not to be an average ass-kicking hero. He's not a Rambo derivative.'

Boone's transformation called for three stages of make-up, each inspired by primitive South American ritual war-paint designs and each more terrifying than the last. Sheffer enjoyed his moments caked in paint and prosthetics and, despite occasional irritations, became enamoured of his creature persona.

'The hardest thing is the hours,' he explains. 'You get here at four in the morning and then by the time six in the evening rolls around you're supposed to start emoting – there's not much left after fourteen hours and not having got much sleep the night before, so that's a little rough.'

Night shoots in the part-built Necropolis on the studio's muddy backlot were complicated by Pinewood's proximity to local housing. As a result, no loud noises, and certainly no explosions, were allowed after a certain time. 'We have rules and regulations about how late to explode stuff and we have to respect that,' explains Barker.

'We weren't allowed to go any later than midnight. There was a fair amount of late-night shooting. When shooting Boone's death we knew we had to shoot before midnight, when a lot of guns were being fired, and then shoot the lead-up to the death afterwards.'

'I don't know whether I would cast me
in one of my own movies.'

David Cronenberg
ACTOR (DECKER)

Although Midian's inhabitants are grotesque, the true monsters of the movie according to Barker are Sheriff William Eigerman and psychotic psychiatrist Philip Decker, whose on-screen murder victims include *Splatterpunk* horror authors John Skipp and Craig Spector, who were in Britain to watch Barker at work and were roped into the film on the pretext of being wasted on camera.

As Decker, the choice of David Cronenberg, whose acting experience amounted to little more than cameos in John Landis's *Into The Night* and his own version of *The Fly,* may seem somewhat eclectic but Barker sees the Canadian director as a natural in the role of Decker. 'You see him in interviews. He's urbane, witty and dry: and then he makes a movie like *The Fly.*

'He struck me as Decker because Decker has a very good social image as a highly paid analyst with nice suits and a nice office. While at the same time he's a mass murderer and nobody knows!'

'Clive had been watching me do a documentary and as I was talking he thought "This could be a psychiatrist, and this could be a psychiatrist with some secrets" and that made him think that I could play Decker,' explains Cronenberg. 'When you read the novel, you know the way that Decker's described and so on – it's not like me at all, physically in particular, but we all know that that's irrelevant for movies.

'We're always going to create something new for the screen anyway, so I didn't worry about that. My response to him was, "Are you sure you wouldn't rather have a real actor instead?" So I was worried for him. I don't know whether I would cast me in one of my own movies.

'But his reasons were solid. I said, "I don't want to come on the set and have you expect that I can do something that I can't. I have very limited experience as an actor." Clive pointed out what was required and why he thought I could handle it, and I thought, "It makes sense." We'll see when the movie comes out whether he was right or not, but I feel very comfortable on set anyway.'

'Having a world-class director on the set, who you are directing, you are wondering all the time whether he is thinking in the back of his head "Why's he putting the camera there?" But David never did that,' recalls Barker. 'He left yesterday after ten weeks on the shoot and I miss him. He was wonderfully supportive to me and gave me a very real sense of how he worked. And when I did have problems he would tend to be there and say, "I have these all the time too and don't pretend they will go away; however many movies you make, they don't". All of which is very reassuring. He was tremendous.'

'I really want very much to be a very good and obedient actor,' says Cronenberg. 'In fact I talked to an actor before I came here and he said, "All you've got to offer are obedience and punctuality." My response to that was, "Well, that's all I have to offer so I'll give them that because I don't have a lot of experience as an actor to fall back on."'

In spite of Cronenberg's relative inexperience as an actor, Barker believes that he slotted well into his role. 'He wrote speeches for himself,' Barker explains. 'He would come in and say "I think Decker should say this. Decker wouldn't do that."

'One day we had a double in for him, because he was just a hand drinking in a bar, and I called up Kieron Phipps, the assistant director, and I said to Kieron, "Call David, I have to know what Dr Decker drinks." And David gave him the answer: he drank Virgin Marys – ice and tomato juice.

'Decker is such a control freak. David pointed out, quite rightly, that he wouldn't drink anything with alcohol in, for fear of letting the dark side go.'

Despite his insight into Decker's character, Cronenberg still had to rely on Barker's direction for the key to his performance. 'As an actor I have to depend on the director for my level. The first scene I did was one that happens right at the end of the movie and that was my introduction to the character of Decker. I don't say a word but it's a very complex scene. Clive had to tell me what level we were on for that because I didn't know.

'He's the only one who has the whole picture in his mind,' says Cronenberg of Barker. 'And my instincts might say do this scene in an hysterical tone and he might say, "No, no, that's quite wrong because you've got to build up later to even more hysteria." So if you go totally to the top you've got no place to go. It's really a discussion, a collaboration.'

This ability to communicate has earned Barker the admiration of his crew. Supervising producer Gabriella Martinelli says: 'Clive has a very fertile imagination. Considering this is his second movie you would think he had the experience of many more under his belt. He very quickly assimilates all the various technical details that you need in film and will learn on the spot something that will take other people a long time to know. He's very talented. There are a lot of directors who can do the job functionally, but he has that extra special edge which makes him stand out.'

Barker's director of photography Robin Vidgeon also shares Martinelli's opinion. 'I did a picture in Italy with Zeffirelli, who's into every single thing on a film set: lenses, camera, lights, costumes, sets, design. He has his touch on everything and Clive is the same. He ducks, he dives, his mind is so fast, it's quite extraordinary to see someone with such enthusiasm.'

Unfortunately, despite the camaraderie amongst the principle players, the crew and their director, Barker is keen to stress that a film studio is not always happy-happy-land.

'Movies are not made by people smiling all the time and having an absolutely wonderful time. I know it's an old cliché to say that the movie business isn't glamorous, but I don't think you can emphasise that strongly enough sometimes. When you were on F Stage, there was smoke and there was fire and there was dirt and it went on for three weeks.

'We'd all cough up gobs of black shit at the end of the day. It's not great. Craig would have been in make-up for six hours. He would come in and he would be pissed off and tired, and he'd come on set to meet a bunch of people who were trying to lay tracks in dirt . . . it was not a great situation.'

The movie's major nightmare occurred on the picture when Christopher Figg, the original producer of *Nightbreed, Hellraiser,* and *Hellbound,* resigned following a row over budgets. After seven hectic weeks of shooting the blow greatly upset Barker and, as he later admitted, it also put his cast and crew into a daze. 'One of the guys who played the Breed happened to be on set the moment that Chris Figg was telling the crew he was leaving, and he said he'd never walked into an atmosphere so thick in his life.

'It was a major moment for the movie, for Figg, for me, and for the dissolution of our business partnership. It was a very, very heavy duty thing to happen seven weeks into a very gruelling shoot. I don't think that can be discounted. It's like *Munchausen.* The story of how *Munchausen* did what it did and cost what it cost has become more important than the movie, and to some extent I think that's true of *The Abyss* as well. The fact that *The Abyss* was made under the most gruelling circumstances known to man becomes more important than the picture itself, and I think that, to some extent, that's to the detriment of the picture.

'I think the problem was that the movie grew. The movie should never have been attempted at its initial scale, and what happened was that we began to be in a situation where we were obliged to chase our own tails just trying to keep up with the amount of work that the movie actually required.'

> 'There must be something of an
> Eigerman in all of us.'
>
> **Charles Haid**
> ACTOR (EIGERMAN)

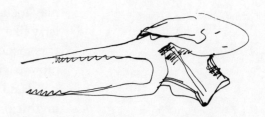

Decker's compatriot in evil is Sheriff William Eigerman, played by Charles Haid who spent the best part of the eighties in uniform as Renko in TV's *Hill Street Blues.* But Haid's initial reluctance to accept another role as a police officer was eventually countered by his desire to work with Barker. 'I was pretty reluctant to take the part,' Haid admits, 'but I did because of Clive.

'We were out having a drink when Danny Elfman (*Nightbreed*'s composer), whose music I admire, showed up. I thought, this is looking pretty interesting, and as Clive went out to go to the john I said to Danny, "What are you doing here?" and he said, "I want to work with this guy, he's a genius." That sort of sold me on it.

'Also, the whole idea of the mythology that he's working from, the good versus the evil, was something that appealed to me. It's got every conflict within this piece here, and the characters are representative of many facets of our natures.

'There was also the chance to play a character with no redeeming qualities whatsoever in Eigerman. I started re-searching those kinds of people and the nature of that kind of person and I came up with an interesting quote. I saw an Academy Award-winning documentary on Klaus Barbie and one of the things he said was "I am the son of the Eiger." Eiger being "rocks" in German and Klaus Barbie being the butcher of Lyons. A man of stone, a man with no heart, a man with no soul, capable of the absolute butchery of humanity.'

Haid has no doubts as to Eigerman's prominence in the downfall of the Breed. His form of fatalism, his need for continuity and hatred of change, is more dangerous than any of Decker's psychotic furies.

'If you want to find the real devil in this piece it's Eigerman and his mentality. So the idea to play that, especially to play a character who would destroy everything that I particularly like as an actor and a person – the wonders of the world – was fascinating. Hopefully, by the end the audience will be more frightened of Eigerman than of any of the monsters.'

Haid became heavily interested in Barker's story and its mythical sub-text, seeing Boone as Christ resurrected, Baphomet as God, and Decker as the Devil. During long, philosophical discussions before and after his stints on set he also interpreted the mythology in terms of Islam, Judaism and fairy tales. 'It's very, very, inter-related. If you look at Mohammed, Islam, Jews, it's always the same kind of stories.'

Barker agrees but stresses that he is not rewriting a particular mythology. 'I am writing about lost tribes. I'm doing something about alternative gods. Boone is Midian's seventh messiah, you see. And finally he gets to save the tribe. Fucks a lot of them over in the meantime, but he does save the tribe.

'Every mythology has elements in common. It's not that one's rewriting the Bible, it's just that one's always interested in hitting the beats that move people. A lot of those beats are about salvation and the coming of messiahs, because those are common to every mythology, not just the Christian mythology. So I'm using those images and ideas but I'm trying to find a new purpose for them.'

'We're here because of Clive Barker.'

Jim Robinson
PRODUCER

Twenty-five sets were built at Pinewood Studios with even the production's office complex dressed up as the interior and exterior of Shere Neck's police station; Eigerman's office was in fact the producer's. For a film set totally in Canada, only one week of shooting actually took place there.

The film's most important sets, however, were Midian's Core and Baphomet's Chamber; both of which were created in Pinewood's massive A-Stage under the guidance of first-time production designer Steve Hardie, who fortunately had Barker's clearly defined images of Midian both in the novel and in his concept drawings to work from.

The Midian set cost £70,000 out of a total art department budget of £250,000 and was filmed on for just two weeks. It is the largest of all the film's sets, a nest of subtly lit caverns laced with rope ladders and a furiously animated band of pacing, fighting, eating creatures. But even with the film's $11 million budget, a modest amount by today's standards, and even more remarkable given *Nightbreed*'s complex mixture of special effects, cost cutting measures were still employed. 'It's not an open cheque to create anything,' laments Hardie. 'So we are building halves of sets which then spin around and constitute the full set, and trying to

work to make things look a lot bigger than they are, with very minimal resources.

'It is quite difficult to try and justify money on something in screen time. It is always the temptation when you've built something which cost a hell of a lot of money to try and keep them in the film. You think, I've spent all this money, I'd better keep it on screen.'

To create the illusion of size within Midian, Hardie and his team had to create a scenic painting on the floor of the soundstage with tiny lightbulbs in the shape of windows and doors to establish perspective.

'Hopefully, with the geography of the place, as you cross the bridges, go down stairs and eventually go into the corridor which leads to the god's Chamber, there is a sense that you go right into the depths of Midian where Baphomet is.'

Hardie, however, feels that money can sometimes cramp creativity. 'A lot of bigger-budget film companies have lost some of the magic and trickery involved in cinema. A lot of people do build sets for real, but we're not making documentaries. There's a lot of cheating, a lot of theatre that can be used to make things look bigger or different to what they are. And what we've built here for the money is visually quite exciting and it's been shot to death, whereas on a huge budget film this would have been built possibly to a higher standard and quality and used only for a few shots. I feel my job is to give Clive what he wants because it's his vision, his book and, unfortunately, a director cannot do it all.'

'He respects your point of view, but
he always wants it his way.'

Julian Parry
ART DIRECTOR

Another person responsible for realising Barker's visions – albeit on a much smaller scale – was model-maker Julian Parry. As a miniatures designer on movies such as *Aliens* and *Willow*, Parry was initially expecting to construct models for *Nightbreed* which would simply allow key sequences – such as the truck plunging into Midian's central core – to be shot without the expense of destroying the real sets.

But when the movie's heads of production wrestled with the problem of breeding realism into the main Midian Core, which, because only half the full-size version had been built, was impossible to use for long shots, Parry found

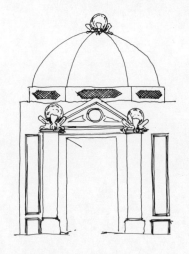

his job had snowballed. 'I told them that I could build and light the whole thing as a model,' explains Parry. 'I went away and did it. They were so pleased with the result that they then allowed me a great deal of freedom to work on all the other models.'

He did not, however, expect to be made art director when 20th Century Fox decided to add three weeks to the production schedule for an enhancement shoot in which three new monsters were created and extra scenes with Lylesburg, Peloquin and Narcisse were shot.

Parry's promotion to art director was only one of a major succession of events that occurred during the hectic final weeks of shooting. Barker was suddenly torn between wrapping the last few scenes and preparing for the arrival of Ralph McQuarrie, Bruce Nyznik, and Danny Elfman, who would add matte paintings, soundtracks and musical score respectively during post-production.

Barker also had to keep an eye on the editing of the movie by industry veteran Richard Marden who, in those final weeks, was joined by James Bond *License to Kill* editor John Grover.

Although not the first horror film he edited, having worked on Tobe Hooper's *Lifeforce,* Grover was astonished by what he initially saw of *Nightbreed* footage. 'It was fascinating to watch, it was an hour and three quarters long, and we didn't take our eyes off the screen. It was completely different. I didn't know what shocking thing was going to happen next.'

Editors must also pace a movie and, as in *License to Kill,* John Grover had to balance graphic violence with suspense and continuing action. 'I was given one of those sequences where the snake comes out of a man's stomach and, of course, I was given about fifteen to twenty slates and just tried to make a sequence out of it. I tried to build it up a bit, but when I see it in context, you don't need to set up the rumbling stomach and see the snakes start, you just want to go bang, bang, and the snakes come out and that's what we've done now.'

Occasionally, Grover's job put him into a benign conflict with Barker because of his aversion to the unnecessary use of bad language. 'I said to Clive that I found one "fuck" in the picture completely unnecessary. He picked that up and he knew immediately that I didn't like it. You have that sort of thing in these pictures for the same reason you have the shocks or the gore, to make people hate it.'

The majority of the editing process is done without the background sounds and music that will accompany the finished film in the cinemas. These were added in the case of *Nightbreed* by Bruce Nyznik and Danny Elfman.

Nyznik housed his hi-tech synthesising equipment in the same building that contained the Nightbreed and, with unearthly wails and screams escaping through its walls day and night, it was with some trepidation that one even approached it.

His computers are able to recreate any sounds programmed into them from samples taken around the world, ranging from barn owls to eerie footsteps, and produce them at a variety of pitch. He runs a film sequence and builds two or maybe even three layers of sound into it.

'The most important thing in any sound effect is what's the heart of it? What is the centre of the poem? What is it really about, and how does it affect the person in it?'

For the scene in which Decker slashes the throat of a woman in the privacy of her own kitchen he picks out a recording of people who have to speak without a larynx. 'It's mucal speech and it's very bizarre and very disturbing. So, in that moment, even though it's brief and fleeting, to me the most important part of the throat-cut isn't the swoosh of the knife, and it isn't really the sound of a knife cutting flesh, because that happens so quickly it's covered in the swoosh. What's important is the person trying to speak. No matter what the music's doing or the other sound effects are doing, somewhere clearly you have to realise that she's trying to speak. And that should break your heart as well as horrify you.'

Picture and soundtrack combine with the musical score to create the finished film and, with Danny Elfman, whose scores for *Beetlejuice* and *Batman* have already won high praise, on the payroll, Barker was confident that he had something special. 'Sound,' explains Barker, 'most people are particularly ignorant of how enriching that can be. Imagine the whole of *Star Wars* without the sounds of machines passing over, and the lasers. The sound adds to the whole disgust level.'

The call for weird and unique sounds fired Bruce with an enthusiasm that even surprised Barker. 'There's a sound buried in the background of the Midian Core,' says Barker. 'And I asked him what it is and he said it's the mating call of an Elk!'

Barker was also hoping to be surprised by Danny Elfman. 'Danny wanted to do a scarey movie. He's got a frenzied imagination. The soundtrack will be very dark and orchestral and there will be one hour of music in the picture. It will be a rich soundtrack as the picture is rich visually.'

Nightbreed's final visual embellishment was achieved when artist Ralph McQuarrie, the veteran designer of most of the hardware in the *Star Wars* movies, was brought in to produce the matte paintings for the Necropolis sequences, help Barker to visualise new monsters for the enhancement shoot, paint a huge mural representing the history of the Breed, and create an early incarnation of the movie's poster.

His paintings of sarcophagi and crypts, when combined with live action shots of the Necropolis, produce the type of panoramic views of the above-ground Midian which would not have been otherwise achieved without a much larger budget; while the new creature designs were used during

CLIVE BARKER'S **NIGHT BREED**

the enhancement shoot. The mural was to be incorporated into the movie's opening sequences.

At the end of the Pinewood shoot, and just days before he flew to America to finish dubbing the movie, an exhausted Clive Barker looked back on the three months of principal photography with a knowing, though not wary, eye. 'The movie has come out so much better than I ever dreamed it would. It's also squeezed out of me so much more energy than I thought it was going to. I went through a very bad period of not just energy-lag but a sense that there was no light at the end of the tunnel and that this would never fucking end.

'Robin Vidgeon has worked with Spielberg, and he's been making movies for a very long time, yet he said to me as he left after the enhancement shoot, that it was the most gruelling film he'd ever been on. Major make-ups, major prosthetics, major special effects – fire, explosions, destruction, end of the universe – all for $11 million. And all the time, not being able to say quite confidently, "Ah, well, this is what we're doing."

'All the time we were trying to find a new way to do stuff,' says Barker, 'and that I think is the greatest challenge. But it does mean that you don't have the clichés to fall back on. You can't say, "Oh well, I don't feel terribly energetic this Monday morning, let's just do it the way that X or Y would have done it." As with always trying to find new ways to do things, once you've started on that track you can't really go back. You're stuck with it.'

Barker already has a sequel in mind if *Nightbreed* is a box-office success, but it has little to do with this step. *Nightbreed II* will continue in directions not immediately apparent from the play of the first.

'Midian is destroyed,' Barker explains, 'and the second movie does not happen minutes later. It happens after the passage of some time. *Nightbreed* leaves a lot of questions unanswered, a lot of long-term questions. The second movie is not what will happen tomorrow.'

Although Decker and Eigerman are obvious choices for the continued onslaught against the Breed, it is Ashberry, the puny young priest played by Malcolm Smith who is the key to the further adventures of Cabal. He is a man twisted by a loss of faith and a liking for alcohol. 'We're not sure why he puts his hand in the potion to change himself at the film's end,' says Smith. 'It seems very predestined. Much greater powers have brought him there.

'He is sent as a messenger from another god, but I don't think we know whether he's good or bad.'

Barker, however, is in no doubt as to Ashberry's future function. 'There are people out there in the world who have been waiting for Ashberry. Just as there are people out there who have been waiting for Boone. Secret orders who have been waiting for their particular Lucifer. Armies waiting to rise who want a leader, and Ashberry is going to walk into their lives like I guess Hitler did; to stir up some deep feeling.'

The story of Cabal and the Nightbreed will continue.

SCREENPLAY

FADE IN:

Scene 1. TITLE SEQUENCE

Darkness. Then, a burst of sparks from a bowl held in a scaly hand. The light shows us a mural. We start to move along the wall. First we see stars and planets, painted in a primitive, stylized fashion on bare rock. A voice on the track speaks softly to us.

VOICE: We did not always live in hiding.

We have come to the image of a huge family tree, which springs from a single seed but divides into two separate halves. On the left, ruled by the moon, the branches blossom into extraordinary creatures. On the right, by sunlight, the branches end in ordinary human beings.

VOICE: Once we roamed the earth freely, born to possess the night as Naturals are born to the day. For we are the tribes of the moon. We are the Nightbreed.

Upon the word *Nightbreed* the title comes up on the screen, against the image of a moon painted on the wall.

SCENES 2–2K DELETED

2L. **EXT.**   REEDS   NIGHT

Cut to a real moon. Then cut wide to a moonlit landscape, through which the camera careens madly. The soundtrack, which was lush and almost sacred in the mural chamber, erupts into a tribal rhythm. We glimpse creatures in the darkness, moving through the reeds. They are barely more than silhouettes. We see teeth, and gleaming eyes; glimpses of naked, patterned flesh. Only glimpses.

2M. **INT.**   MURAL CHAMBER

Cut back to the mural chamber. Now we have moved away from the tree to a more brutal scene. A symbolic representation of a great apocalyptic war between Naturals and Breed. Terrible scenes of destruction.

VOICE: But the Naturals made war on us. They feared us for our strength. They envied our powers. They called us monsters, killing us by whatever means their malice could invent, finding in each of us our particular vulnerability.

We are scanning scenes of that war. A Breed being staked like a vampire. Another being shot like a werewolf. Another exposed to sunlight.

VOICE: None of us was safe. The tribes of the moon dwindled. Our gods were slaughtered, our homes destroyed. It was the Apocalypse.

2N.   **EXT.**   NECROPOLIS WALL AND GATES

Cut back to the landscape. The clouds roil above the heads of the creatures heading through the reeds. We see their destination now. A huge wall, with gates.

2P.   **INT.**   MURAL CHAMBER

And back to the mural chamber, and a final scene. The gates we've just seen are in the painting. Looking over them, calling the Breed in, is a vast, indistinct form: that of Baphomet. His eyes burn; his arms are open in welcome.

VOICE: Only one of our Gods survived the holocaust. Baphomet. Wounded and near to death, he summoned us, the last of the last, into hiding. Into Midian, where we wait now. The battle is over but not the war. There will come a saviour.

Now we've moved beyond the image of the gate into a new patch of wall on which the pictures are only vague sketches. We can interpret some of the images nevertheless: a man with a bloody hole in the middle of his chest. A man wearing a mask like a skull. We linger on a faceless figure.

VOICE: His name is Cabal. He will lead and give us back the Night. We are the tribes of the moon. We are the Nightbreed.

The titles end.

2Q. **EXT.**   NECROPOLIS WALL AND GATES

Cut back to the landscape. Now we are at the gates, and the creatures slip through and away into the mist. Only one, a beautiful, ferocious female called Shuna Sassi remains, turning to look at us. She beckons.

SHUNA: Come . . .

The camera retreats from her.

SHUNA: Will you not come?

Now the last of the creatures, the Drummer, takes her by the arm, snatching her away through the gates. As she disappears, the camera follows again, stopping at the gates themselves, which close with an unearthly din.

CUT TO:

2R. **INT.**   LORI'S APARTMENT   NIGHT

C.U. on Boone, closed eyes. He is dreaming. His gaze roves beneath his lids.
  Lori's lips come into shot, kissing first his eyes and then travelling down his face to his mouth.

  LORI: Boone . . . wake up.

Boone's eyes flicker open.

  LORI: Hi. You OK?
  BOONE: Yep.

Now Boone's eyes are fully open. He sits up. Looks towards the open window. Night beyond. She kisses him, distracting him from the sight of the window.

  LORI: You want something to eat?
  BOONE: Sure. What time is it?
  LORI: Nine-thirty. I was letting you doze.
  BOONE: Thought you'd worn me out, huh?

Lori smiles, and kisses him, then crosses the room to the kitchen area, picks up some fruit, and a knife, carrying both back to where Boone is lying on the bed. It is unmade. Both Lori and Boone are lightly dressed, clothes casually thrown on after an afternoon of lovemaking.

LORI: You know what?
BOONE: What?
LORI: We should get out of Calgary for a few days. Just take off.
BOONE: Anywhere special?
LORI: Somewhere we can be alone together.
BOONE: More alone than this?
LORI: Yeah. Just you and me. No work. No telephone calls. No . . .
BOONE: Bad dreams.
LORI: No bad dreams.
BOONE: How did you know?
LORI: I know. I always know. It's no big deal.
BOONE: I'm going around with some crazy loop in my head.
LORI: You're not crazy.
BOONE: No.
LORI: Say it like you believe it.
BOONE: I believe it. I'm not crazy. But I want this damn dream out of my head.

He gets up and goes to the window.

BOONE: Decker's started calling me again.

LORI: When?

BOONE: All last week. Every day.

LORI: What does he want?

BOONE: I don't know, I haven't called him back.

LORI: If he can help, see him. Tell him it's all gone but for the bad dreams.

BOONE: They're not bad. That's what's weird. The more I have them the more I like them. Now I *do* sound like a crazy, right?

LORI: No. You sound like the man I love. A little haunted, maybe, but the sanest man I ever met.

BOONE: Keep going.

LORI: Will you see Decker?

BOONE: You think I should?

LORI: Where's the harm? You tell him from me, I'm the only thing you should be dreaming about.

BOONE: I don't think he'd get it. He never had a wet dream in his life.

LORI: I don't want to be competing with things I can't see, Boone. Can't share. I don't want to be always feeling that something's pulling at you.

BOONE: I'm not going anywhere, Lori. Except with you.

LORI: I can't hear that often enough.

BOONE: I'll never leave you. Not ever. I swear.

He kisses her, passionately.

BOONE: Can't remember a time when I didn't love you.

LORI: How about before you met me?

BOONE: Even then.

They kiss again. We move past them into the darkness outside the window.

Dissolve to the moon, clearing cloud.

SCENES 3–15 DELETED

16. **EXT.**   RICKMAN HOUSE   NIGHT

A pleasant house in a pleasant neighbourhood. Lights burn inside.

17. **INT.**   RICKMAN HOUSE   NIGHT

Melissa Rickman emerges from the lounge, with a Dagwood sandwich, a work in progress. She is thirty-five, and going to seed in a gentle way. Her husband, Lou Rickman, a similar type, is planted in front of the television.

MELISSA: Okay, you want ham, cheese, pickle, mustard?

LOU: All of the above and a brewski, thank you.

MELISSA: You're getting porky, Lou.

LOU [amiable – tries to grab her]: I'm comfortable. I like myself fat. I like you fat too . . .
MELISSA [secretly amused – she hushes him]: Keep it down, Lou, you'll wake the munchkins.

She hears something upstairs, goes to the foot of the stairs, looks up. Her eldest son, Lou Two, waddles into view. He's five.

LOU TWO: Mommy . . .
MELISSA: Sweetie, you're supposed to be beddy-bye.
LOU TWO: I heard something.
MELISSA: What did you hear, honey?
LOU TWO: Bad man.
MELISSA: No, everything's okay. You go back to bed, munchkin, I'll be up to see you in a minute.
LOU [V.O.]: How's that sandwich coming?
MELISSA: Coming . . .

Melissa disappears from the bottom of the stairs.

18. **INT.**   RICKMAN KITCHEN   NIGHT

Melissa enters, moves out of sight. We stay at the door. A figure appears dressed in black, knives in both hands, and crosses to leave the screen again. We do not see his face. But we hear his labours: the sound of the blades slicing Melissa. She staggers into view, grabbing hold of her slit throat. Blood bubbles between her fingers. The figure appears behind her. She turns, as the knife descends.

19. **INT.**   RICKMAN LOUNGE   NIGHT

Lou hears a sound, rises and moves towards the kitchen door.

LOU: Melissa?

At the top of the stairs, Lou Two watches wide-eyed.

20. **INT.**   RICKMAN STAIRS   NIGHT

Lou Two's P.O.V. – We see blood running along the hallway.

21. **INT.**   RICKMAN KITCHEN   NIGHT

Lou reaches the kitchen door and sees Melissa laid out, dead, on the kitchen table.

LOU: Oh God – GOD!

Lou enters, the figure emerges from behind him. While we remain at the door watching, detached, Lou fights back, throwing himself back and forth around the kitchen. But the figure is much stronger. We glimpse its face now, it is a mask, with a zipper for a mouth and buttons for eyes, blank. Devoid of compassion, hatred or regret. A death's head, made by a mad child.

Atop the stairs, Lou Two listens. His baby sister cries in her cot. He looks her way then back downstairs. The sounds cease. Silence. Terror on his face. Then the child's perfect nightmare appears at the bottom of the stairs. The figure, heavy knife in hand, starts to climb, dragging Lou's bloody body after him by the hair.

DISSOLVE TO:

22.   SCENE DELETED

22A.   **INT.**   BOONE'S APARTMENT   NIGHT

Empty. The phone rings. We move towards the answering machine, which clicks on.

BOONE [on tape]: Hi. Please leave a message.
LORI [thru phone]: Boone, pick up will you? Boone? Are you there? Boone? Okay, so don't answer. See you tomorrow . . . G'night.

23.   SCENE DELETED

24.   **EXT.**   RICKMAN HOUSE   NIGHT

Three patrol cars, an ambulance, policemen restraining a small crowd gathered outside. An n.d. sedan roars up, red bubble light flashing, and Inspector Joyce gets out and moves towards the house. He's greeted by the Medical Examiner, Dr Burton, just exiting, carrying a medical bag.

BURTON [bitter]: Brace yourself, Inspector.
JOYCE: Same profile?
BURTON: Unmistakable. Doesn't miss a trick.
JOYCE [anguished]: Kids? Two kids?
BURTON: If it's any comfort, they went quickly.
JOYCE: Yeah. Makes me feel a whole lot better about the sick fuck.
BURTON: Find this guy, Joyce. They say these guys want to be caught. I think this one likes it too much.

A rookie patrolman stands on the doorstep, on the verge of tears.

JOYCE [gently]: Let's get these tourists back, Officer.
POLICEMAN: Yes sir.
JOYCE [to Burton]: If we can't protect the kids, what the hell use are we?

25. SCENE DELETED

26. **EXT.**   SUNRISE

The sun climbs above the horizon, behind the cityscape of Calgary.
Another day begins.

27. SCENE DELETED

28. SCENE DELETED

29. **INT.**   DR DECKER'S OFFICE   DAY

Close on a pile of tapes, marked with dates over a period of two years. They're on Decker's desk.

> DECKER: I've been listening to the tapes of our sessions. All two years' worth . . .

We move from the tapes to Decker, who gets up from his desk and moves around to the other side. Boone is sitting on the other side of the desk, his posture far from relaxed. He hates this room. As Decker moves, we take in the various pictures on the walls. Dance pictures, photographs of Decker with civic dignitaries, crippled children etc.

> BOONE: Why?
> DECKER: Most of my colleagues would have walked away from a case like yours. The most they would have done was drug you. But you . . . you intrigued me. All the talk of monsters. And Midian. Remember Midian?
> BOONE: That wasn't me. I heard about Midian from other people.
> DECKER: But you made it part of your private mythology.
> BOONE: I suppose I did. It was a place of refuge.
> DECKER: When you imagined yourself being taken off to this invented city, to Midian, what crimes were you going to be forgiven?

Boone's looking uneasy now. He wipes sweat from his upper lip.

BOONE: You know what I used to dream.

DECKER: Yes. There's a remarkable consistency in the images you see. Great detail. Almost as though the violence was *real*.

BOONE: They were just bad dreams. Midian doesn't exist. Monsters don't exist.

DECKER: But murder does, Boone. Murder's very real. It may start in the mind, but it ends up changing to flesh and blood.

He picks up the envelope we saw in his previous scene, and takes the photographs out.

DECKER [cont.]: Two days ago the police brought me some photographs. They wanted to know if I had any patients who might be capable of what's in these photographs. I'm going to show you them. Are you ready for that?

Boone nods.

Decker lays the photographs on the table. Boone picks them up. We get glimpses of what they contain. Domestic horrors. Bloody scenes of corpses caught by the camera in grotesque positions, sliced up and bleeding. Boone's breath quickens.

DECKER [cont.]: When you talk about murder on the tapes, I thought it was invention. Now I'm not so sure.

Boone keeps staring at the pictures. The glassy eyes stare hard at him. His breathing is now rapid and shallow. One or two of the images seem to *move.* Bodies twitch. He drops the photographs.

BOONE: I didn't . . .
DECKER: Didn't what?
BOONE: They were bad dreams.
DECKER: What you describe in your sessions is very specific. Houses; faces . . .
BOONE: I don't remember.
DECKER: You want to hear?
BOONE: No!

Decker picks up the photographs. Boone, highly agitated, gets up and paces the room.

BOONE [cont.]: You think I did this?
DECKER: Six families killed over a two-year period. All within driving distance of Calgary . . .
BOONE [fury]: Do you think I did this?
DECKER: I hope to God you didn't, for both our sakes. We've come a long way together. I don't want to believe this any more than you do.
BOONE: But you do.
DECKER: I wouldn't put us through this pain if I didn't . . . if I wasn't . . . afraid you had.
BOONE [desperate; helpless]: What do I do? God, tell me what to do.
DECKER: I can only go so far on your behalf. Patient confidentiality's one thing. Protecting a killer is another.
BOONE [breaking down]: Jesus . . . Jesus . . . Jesus . . .

Decker returns to his desk. Puts the photographs down and picks up a vial of prescription pills. He crosses to Boone.

DECKER: Listen to me. Take these, they'll help. Go home, and consider what we've talked about. I'm going to give you twenty-four hours to go to the police and answer their questions of your own accord. That's as long as I can give you. If you haven't complied by then, I'm afraid I'll have to tell them what I know.

Boone grabs the pills.

DECKER [cont.]: I can't tell you how sorry I am . . .

30. SCENE DELETED

31. SCENE DELETED

SCENES 32, 33 DELETED

34. **INT.**   DECKER'S BUILDING HALLWAY   DAY

Boone exits into the hall, forces open the vial of pills, swallows a couple, shaking, trying to control his terror.

35. **INT.**   DECKER'S OFFICE   DAY

Decker sits at his desk, lifts his briefcase, opens it, tosses the folder of photographs into the case. Looking into the case he seems on the verge of some powerful emotion. Rage? Revulsion? He snaps shut the briefcase. The emotion passes.

36. **INT.**   BOONE'S APARTMENT   DAY

Boone enters the apartment, his eyes wild. He slams the door and closes his eyes.

SHOCK CUT TO:

36A. MURDER PHOTOGRAPHS/BOONE'S HALLUCINATION

Boone studies the photographs in his hand, and they come to life.

37. SCENE DELETED

38. SCENE DELETED

38A. **INT.**   BOONE'S APARTMENT   DAY

Boone opens his eyes.

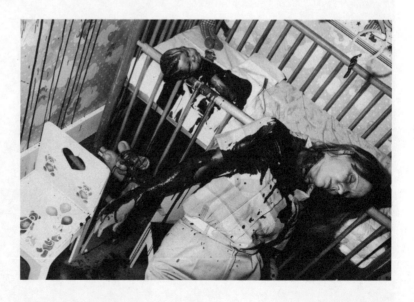

39. SCENE DELETED

39A. **INT.**   BOONE'S BATHROOM   DAY

Boone chews the pills. He is now sweating and shaking violently.
   Boone strips off his clothes.

40. SCENE DELETED

40A. **INT.**   BOONE'S APARTMENT   AFTERNOON

Boone opens his drawers and pulls out photographs, his passport
etc and starts to make a pile with them. He pours lighter fuel on the
pictures, and watches them burn. Sitting against the wall still
sweating he takes more pills.
   We see Lori's love letters burn and hear her voice speaking the
words as they are consumed.
   Boone cries. Then he hears Lori's voice say:

   LORI: Boone . . .

Lori is sitting on the edge of the bed. Boone looks round, sees
himself against the wall and moves forward past the real Boone
towards the bed . . .
   Boone watches as he and Lori make love on the bed. We close in
on the love-making. Lori leans to kiss him.

   BOONE: I'll never leave you . . .

Cut back to Boone, his face all grief.

   BOONE: Stupid.

Boone's
Hallucination:

                                        CUT TO:

40B. **INT.**   BOONE'S BATHROOM   AFTERNOON

Boone's hand pulls the shower curtain aside and turns on the
water. The water pours on him.

41. HALLUCINATION

Another of the murder scenes comes to life. Corpses pulse with
hideous animation.

42. **INT.**   BOONE'S BATHROOM   AFTERNOON

With a cry Boone slides to the shower floor, panting, haunted,
destroyed.

   BOONE [faintly]: . . . I did it . . . I did it all . . .

43. **INT.**   BOONE'S APARTMENT   EVENING

Behind him, the last of the fire flickers. He looks through the blinds at the sunset. Takes another pill. Puts on his leather jacket. Exits. The door slams.

44. SCENE DELETED

45. **INT.**   NIGHTCLUB   NIGHT

Lori is on stage, sexy, vivacious, fronting a tight C & W band in a hip rendition of 'Johnny Be Angry'.

46. **INT.**   NIGHTCLUB   NIGHT

Lori's P.O.V. looking through the crowd in front of the stage. Lori spots Boone standing near the entrance, his face in shadow.
    Her eyes light up with joy as the song builds to climax. It ends. Applause, cat whistles, foot stomping. Lori's in heaven. She looks out again.
    Boone is gone.

47. **EXT.**   HIGHWAY   NIGHT

Boone steps into view by the side of the road, watches the traffic.

INTERCUT:

48. **INT.**   NIGHTCLUB CORRIDOR   NIGHT

Confused and worried, Lori stands in the empty corridor, a note Boone has left for her in her hand.

Boone edges out closer to the road. Spots a huge semi with a fully loaded trailer barrelling down towards him.

Lori opens the note and reads: *'Keep this. Burn the rest. All wrong.'* Tears burst from Lori's eyes.

Boone flings himself in front of the oncoming truck.

CUT TO BLACK:
FADE IN:

49. **INT.**   HOSPITAL EMERGENCY ROOM   NIGHT

A blaze of light. A bustling emergency receiving area. A stern nurse goes through the pockets of Boone's jacket, which is lying beside him on a gurney. His eyes are closed, face and T-shirt bloody. She fishes out the vial of pills.

Boone moans, opens his eyes.

NURSE: Lucky you're in one piece, fella.
BOONE [realizing where he is]: . . . can't even kill myself . . .
NURSE: There's a cheerful thought. [to an approaching doctor] I don't know what kind of fuel he's using, but this guy's cruising at about 35,000 feet.

The doctor takes the vial of pills, checks the label. Opens Boone's eyes, shines a pinlight flash on the pupils. Boone recoils. Doctor takes his pulse.

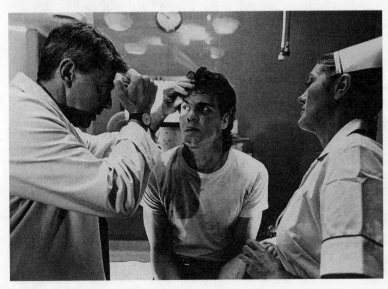

DOCTOR: You don't hit that altitude on lithium carbonate. Let's get the prescribing doctor on the line . . . [finally – to Boone] Okay, we're doing all right, aren't we? Tell me, what've you been taking tonight, partner?

BOONE: Lithium . . .

The doctor opens the vial, looks at a handful of the pills.

DOCTOR: Lithium? This isn't lithium, my friend. [to the nurse] Let's move him. Observation, let's get an IV, valium/saline, 200 milligrams percodan for pain, as needed . . . [quietly – hands the pills to the nurse] We'll have to call this in.

She nods. With considerable effort, Boone sits up urgently and grabs the doctor's hand, holding the pills.

BOONE: What was I taking?

DOCTOR [patronizing]: Easy. We won't know until we run some tests. Looks like some kind of lab quality psychotropic hallucinogen. You're on what we used to call a 'bad trip' there, buddy. You relax now, you're gonna be fine.

The doctor and nurse ease Boone back down onto the gurney. The doctor moves away. The nurse pulls back the curtain and rolls Boone across the hall into a semi-private room.

50. **INT.**   SEMI-PRIVATE HOSPITAL ROOM   NIGHT

From emergency behind them, a warning buzzer sounds.

    VOICE [thru loudspeaker]: Code blue! Code blue!

In an emergency room cubicle, a patient is having a seizure. The nurse rushes off, leaving Boone. Interns roll the cardiac cart toward the cubicle and curtains close around the scene.
    The door to Boone's room swings closed, shutting out the sounds. Boone exhales heavily. Closes his eyes.

    NARCISSE [V.O.] [muttering – half mumbled ranting]: Shit! Shit! Take me, why won't you take me?

Boone opens his eyes. Looks across the room at Narcisse, a wild man, half-derelict, half-punk, bloodied, his hand bandaged, pacing back and forth like a caged cat, staring out of a large picture window at the night.

51. **EXT.**   HOSPITAL WINDOW   NIGHT

Looking in at the brightly lit window framed in the dark building, as Narcisse restlessly moves across it, peering outside.

52. **INT.**   SEMI-PRIVATE HOSPITAL ROOM   NIGHT

    NARCISSE [low and anxious]: They've gone, they've gone, they were here, they were coming for me, where'd they go? Shit!
    BOONE: Hey . . .
    NARCISSE [turns on him – viciously]: Shut up, shut up! They saw you, they won't come while you're here, they won't show themselves to the likes of you, don't you see that?
    BOONE [placating – knows the type]: Sure, okay.
    NARCISSE: Shit! I've missed them, I've missed them! You scared them off, you kept them from me!

Narcisse paces again, starting to sob and sniffle. Boone leans back.

    NARCISSE [cont.] [barely audible – between cries]: . . . Midian . . . Midian . . .

Boone's eyes open like a shot.

    BOONE: What did you say?
    NARCISSE: I said shut up, you want to ruin everything?

Boone leaps to his feet, grabs and easily overpowers the smaller man.

> BOONE: What did you say, just now?
> NARCISSE [suddenly friendly]: What did you say, just now?
> BOONE: You said Midian.
> NARCISSE [coyly]: Did I? Maybe . . .
> BOONE [hurting him – desperate]: What do you know about it?
> NARCISSE: It's where the monsters go. It takes away the pain . . .

Narcisse reaches his hands into his pockets, then comes out with long, silver, razor-sharp artificial nails, curved like hooks, attached to his thumbs. He holds them right at Boone's throat, ready to cut. He smiles.

> NARCISSE [cont.]: . . . what do you know about it?
> BOONE [pause; cautiously]: They forgive you there.
> NARCISSE: Uh-huh. Ever killed anybody?
> BOONE: Yes.
> NARCISSE: See, they only take you if you're worthy. You know what they do to those who aren't worthy?

Boone shakes his head. Narcisse draws one razor-nail lightly across his own throat. A thin trickle of blood runs down his neck. He chuckles.

> BOONE: It's real. Midian's real. [Narcisse nods; carefully] And you know . . . where it is. Don't you? We could go there . . .
> NARCISSE: They sent you. They sent you to take me.
> BOONE: That's right. But first I need to know . . . you have to tell me . . . where it is.
> NARCISSE: It's a test? [Boone nods; Narcisse leans in to him – whispers] No maps.
> BOONE: But you do know. Don't you?
> NARCISSE [looks around; leans in again]: North of Athabasca. East of Peace River. Near Shere Neck, north of Dwyer.

Satisfied, Boone releases him, goes back to the bed, collects his jacket.

> NARCISSE [cont.] [exhilarated]: You'll take me with you, I'm worthy, you ask anyone, I knew you'd come, they sent you to take me, I was waiting. I know, I know, first I have to show you, that's how it works.

Boone is looking out of the window in the door, sizing up his escape.

> BOONE: Show me what?
> NARCISSE: My true face. That's what these are for. [he raises his bladed thumbs] So you can see. I'm not a natural man. Under-

neath I'm a monster, that's how it works; I show you, then you take me with you . . .

He puts the blade to either side of his face. We hear the skin pop.

BOONE: NO!

Blood pours from Narcisse's face, as he traces the outline of his face.

53. **INT.**   EMERGENCY ROOM   NIGHT

Dr Decker, who's just arrived with Lieutenant Joyce and two policemen, is speaking with the doctor that examined Boone.

DECKER [urgent – showing Boone's file]: . . . he was an abandoned child, raised by the state, first diagnosis of incipient schizophrenia at thirteen, juvenile delinquency, periodically

institutionalized through early adulthood . . . some violent episodes, never criminally charged as an adult, he's been in my care for less than a year . . .

A bloodcurdling scream from the semi-private room rivets the attention of the emergency room.

54. **EXT.**   SEMI-PRIVATE ROOM   NIGHT

Following the nurse and an intern as they burst into the room and are greeted with the sight of Narcisse, blood running freely, ripping the last of his scalp off his bare skull, laughing and crying maniacally.

Boone stands near the door, horrified.

> NARCISSE [variously]: TAKE ME! TAKE ME! I'M A MONSTER!
> NURSE [over – to Boone]: What the hell have you done?
> BOONE: Nothing!
> INTERN: Fucking junkies! [at the door – yelling into the corridor] Doctor!

As the door swings open, Boone looks out into the corridor and at the far end of the emergency room he sees Decker and the cops looking his way. Medical support move towards the room, as the nurse and intern try to contain the ranting Narcisse.
    Boone grabs a loose doctor's coat off the back of the door, slips it on and backs out of the room.

> BOONE: Let's get some help in here!

Pandemonium. Narcisse screams, as a half-dozen people struggle to subdue him. As help continues to rush into the room, Boone slowly backs away, out and around a corner. He stops beside a swinging door, sensing something.

55. **EXT.**   SEMI-PRIVATE ROOM   NIGHT

Dr Decker moving through emergency towards the mêlée, stops on the other side of the swinging door, his senses lit up with alarm. He slowly turns to the door. Pushes it open. Empty.

56. **EXT.**   HOSPITAL   NIGHT

Boone moves rapidly away from the exit into the parking lot, tossing off the white coat, breaking into a run. He tries several car doors, finds one open, gets in.

57. **INT.**   CAR   NIGHT

With a rush of focused adrenal intensity, Boone expertly rips open an under panel of the dash, locates and patches together the correct ignition wires and hot-starts the car. Closes the door. Puts it in gear.

58. **EXT.**   HOSPITAL PARKING LOT
     INT.   CAR   NIGHT

Boone slowly drives out of the lot, trying not to attract the attention of the fleet of patrol cars, sirens wailing, pouring into the area.

DISSOLVE TO:

59. **EXT.**   FREEWAY   NIGHT

Boone drives up an entrance ramp and onto the highway, past a sign that reads:

'HIGHWAY 2/NORTH'

DISSOLVE TO:

60. **INT.**   HOSPITAL EMERGENCY WARD   NIGHT

Dr Decker, a few policemen and medical personnel wait outside the door leading to the semi-private room. Lieutenant Joyce exits and a surgeon follows a moment later.

DECKER: What's he saying?
JOYCE: He's talking but he's not making any sense. Something about a place called Midian.
SURGEON: He's dying. I think he wants to die.

Pause. The surgeon moves on.

DECKER [unobtrusively – to Joyce]: Lieutenant, I know Boone. I know how he talks, how he manipulates. Perhaps if the right thing is said to this man it'll trigger something . . .
JOYCE [considers]: No harm in trying.
DECKER: I'll do my best. But I'll need privacy.

Decker enters the room.

61. **EXT.**   SEMI-PRIVATE ROOM   NIGHT

Looking in through the window, we see Decker cross the room to the bed where Narcisse is lying. Decker says something to the nurse. She exits. Decker moves closer to the bed. He reaches into his pocket for something and moves out of our sight.

62. **EXT.**   HIGHWAY/**INT.**   CAR   NIGHT/DAY

Montage – Boone drives through the night, and the following day, through a landscape which becomes increasingly more desolate.

DISSOLVE TO:

63. **EXT.**   ROAD SIGN   LATE AFTERNOON

The road sign reads:

'DWYER – 56 MILES'

Boone's car speeds past.

DISSOLVE TO:

64. **EXT.**   DIRT ROAD OUTSIDE MIDIAN   DAY

Boone's car rolls to a stop. Boone steps out and looks at something in the dust. A battered sign. It reads:

'MIDIAN/POPULATION 63'

There is no sign of life.

BOONE: No . . . oh no . . . [in despair] No!

His shout echoes. The wind blows up a cloud of dust around him. He walks through the dust, on the verge of tears. And then . . . the dust clears, and he sees . . .

INTERCUT:

Necropolis, lying on the other side of a thick expanse of reeds.

Puzzlement overtakes despair. He squints to see more clearly . . .

The Necropolis is vast. High walls, surrounded by reeds, with the tops of mausoleums showing above it. Almost a fortressed town.

Boone starts towards it.

66. **EXT.**   NECROPOLIS GATES   DAY

The sun is low in the sky, the light golden, glinting off the gates. The reeds sigh. Boone pushes one of the gates open and steps inside. His footsteps echo, unnaturally loud in this city of the dead. To either side of him, elegant and elaborate mausoleums, running away into the distance, with numerous smaller tombs set around and between them.

The sun finally sinks out of sight. Its final glow dies on the tops of the mausoleums. There are already stars overhead.

Boone walks on a little way, as the night sounds begin. Exhausted, he sits down on a tomb and leans back against the stone.

BOONE [softly – a bitter irony]: Dead . . . all of the dead . . .

He rummages for a cigarette in his jacket pocket. Pulls one out. Lights it. The flame seems to excite sounds around him. He looks up. The walkways are empty in both directions.

There's a guttural sound at his back. He stands, drops the cigar-

ette, backs away. From the darkness behind him steps a huge form. A knife is put to his lower belly. Its wielder, Kinski, is a massive man, face distorted, his features grotesquely bifurcated.

KINSKI [whispers]: Move and I gut you.

Boone stays still. The growling from between the tombs becomes words.

VOICE [from the darkness]: You got him?
KINSKI: I got him.

A reptilian hand reaches out and picks up Boone's dropped cigarette.

BOONE: Midian? Are you from Midian?
KINSKI: We should take him below, Peloquin.

The silhouette of Peloquin, a were-creature, moves between the tombs. He draws on the cigarette. By its brightening point we glimpse an extraordinary face: more animal than human, but no recognizable species.

PELOQUIN: He's not Nightbreed. He's Natural.
BOONE: No! I've killed people, I'm like you, that's why I'm here . . .
PELOQUIN: Shut the fuck up. You're meat.
KINSKI: If we eat him we break the Law.

BOONE: My God . . . my God, it's true . . .

PELOQUIN: Of course it's true. Everything's true . . . [he starts to emerge from the shadows] God's an astronaut. Oz is over the rainbow. And Midian's where the monsters live. And you came to die.

BOONE: I didn't . . . didn't come to die. I came to be with you, I'm one of you.

Peloquin reaches out and touches Boone's chest.

PELOQUIN: No. Sorry. I can smell innocence at fifty yards.

BOONE: I've killed people. Fifteen people.

PELOQUIN: Who told you that?

BOONE: What do you mean?

PELOQUIN: He lied, asshole. He lied. You're a Natural. And that means . . . you're meat for the Beast.

Peloquin growls, throwing his head back and forth with a strange grace, the image flickering as he does so. Boone watches, amazed. In the blur of Peloquin's motion he transforms, the tentacles on his head lengthening and thickening, thrashing around as though they have a life of their own.

He moves towards Boone, taking hold of him and tearing his T-shirt open.

KINSKI: We mustn't. It's the Law. They'll exile us . . .
PELOQUIN: Fuck the Law! I want meat!

He bites Boone's neck, tearing at his flesh.

KINSKI: Peloquin, no!

Kinski takes the knife from Boone's belly and pushes Peloquin aside. Boone slips away from them.

PELOQUIN: Damn you!

He races after Boone, who runs blindly, his hand pressed to the wound on his neck.

66A. **EXT.**   NECROPOLIS   NIGHT

The Breed listen. We track running feet past the grille, and move close into grille, dropping through a dark rock face.

67. SCENE DELETED

67A. **INT.**   BELOW MIDIAN

In the deep darkness faces look up. The faces are strange and freakish. There is a woman locked in the embrace of a dark monster. A monstrous baby cries.

68. **EXT.**   NECROPOLIS   NIGHT

Boone takes refuge against a mausoleum wall. He takes his hand from the wound on his neck. It is throbbing like a living thing, spreading across his muscle. He stares down at the wound, then touches it lightly. It gives him pleasure.

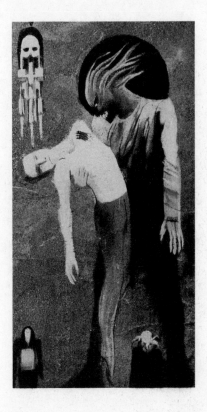

A sound above him. He looks up. Peloquin is climbing down the mausoleum wall, mouth opened wide to take off Boone's head. Boone throws himself forward as the jaws snap shut, missing him by inches. He runs. Kinski appears in his path. For an instant, Boone thinks the game's up . . .

KINSKI: That way! The gate's that way!

Boone sprints.

69. **INT.**   BELOW MIDIAN

The monsters watch and listen.

70. **EXT.**   NECROPOLIS GATES   NIGHT

Peloquin pushes Kinski aside and pelts after Boone, who is at the gate. He flings himself through, and slams it behind him. Peloquin is at the gate, when Kinski comes up behind and restrains him.

KINSKI: He's gone, give it up! You don't dare go out there!

Peloquin stares at Boone through the gate. Panting, sweating, Boone stares back. Snorting with frustration, Peloquin recedes, he and Kinski disappear into shadow.
Boone heaves a sigh of relief, turns from the gate and trudges away into the darkness, when suddenly . . .

71. **EXT.**   OUTSIDE NECROPOLIS GATES   NIGHT

Harsh lights hit Boone from every side; police cars in the reeds all around, their searchlights focused on him. Two dozen cops, all levelling firearms.

Row of headlights ahead —

JOYCE: Freeze! Right there!

Boone squints against the glare.

JOYCE [cont.]: Aaron Boone, you're under arrest. Hands on your head! NOW!

Boone takes a step back. The wound on his neck throbs and swells. At the edge of the light, Decker appears, stepping towards him.

DECKER: Boone, listen to him, it's no use!
JOYCE [to Decker]: Stay back!
DECKER [lowers his voice]: Lieutenant, I can bring him out. He'll listen to me.

Joyce ponders, then signals him forward. Decker advances towards Boone.

DECKER [cont.]: Boone, it's all right, I've explained everything to them.

Rifles are cocked on every side. Decker stops a safe distance from Boone.

DECKER [cont.]: They won't harm you, I give you my word.
BOONE [hanging back]: I didn't do it. I didn't hurt anyone . . .
DECKER [lowering his voice]: Of course you didn't.
BOONE: You . . . you believe me?
DECKER: You wouldn't hurt a fly. [extends a hand] Come on, Boone. It's safe, I've seen to that.
BOONE [taking a tentative step forward]: What, what about the pills?
DECKER [pause; whispers]: What about them, Boone?
BOONE: They weren't tranquillizers . . .

A look of alarm crosses Decker's face. Boone reads it. He gets the picture.

BOONE [cont.]: You set me up . . . you bastard, you set me up!

He lunges for Decker, who turns and throws himself to the ground as he yells.

DECKER: He's got a gun!
JOYCE: FIRE!

The bullets fly. Boone is about to pounce on Decker when he's hit by a barrage, thrown back, riddled with bullets. On the ground, Decker covers his head. Boone goes down. The volley ends.

72. **EXT.** NECROPOLIS NIGHT

The sound of gunfire echoes through the walkways.

73. **INT.** BELOW MIDIAN

In the shadows, a baby held in the arms of a woman with monstrous but beautiful features, begins to cry.

74. **EXT.** OUTSIDE MIDIAN NIGHT

Joyce hears the sound of crying and looks up. Boone's body lies on the ground. Decker rises, hearing the distant sobs on the wind.

75. **INT.** BELOW MIDIAN

The mother hushes the child, her arms, which are tentacles, wrapping around it.

76. **EXT.** OUTSIDE MIDIAN NIGHT

The sound of crying is lost. Joyce moves forward, towards Decker and Boone.

    JOYCE [trying to convince himself]: . . . just the wind.

He reaches Decker, looks down at Boone's body. Looks around.

    JOYCE [cont.]: Where's the gun?
    DECKER [seemingly dismayed]: He reached into his jacket . . . I thought I saw it, I swear . . . oh God, Boone . . .
    JOYCE [quietly, to some cops, meaning Boone]: Get him outta here.

77. **EXT.** NECROPOLIS NIGHT

We track towards a tomb, on which the epitaph reads:

'GOD IS MERCIFUL'

FADE OUT:
FADE IN:

78. **INT.** MORGUE/VIEWING ROOM NIGHT

Moving with Lori, flanked by Dr Burton the pathologist, and a grim Joyce. They enter a smaller room. Burton flips a switch. Curtains part in front of a thick glass panel, revealing a small, sterile viewing chamber.
    In the chamber are a morgue attendant and, lying on a stainless steel table, Boone's body. Lori looks at the body with heartbreaking

sadness. She nods. Burton closes the curtains. Lori and Joyce exit.

On the other side of the glass, the attendant rolls Boone on the table towards a door marked 'Pathology'.

79. **INT.**   INTERVIEW ROOM   NIGHT

Dr Decker sits alone, looking into his briefcase. The door opens, Lori and Joyce enter. Decker closes the briefcase, rises, aggrieved, takes both of Lori's hands in his, speaks soothingly.

> DECKER: Lori, I'm Dr Decker. Boone was my patient.
> LORI: Yes. Hello.
> DECKER: I'm so sorry for your loss. I must tell you, you meant the world to Aaron. He spoke of you constantly . . .
> LORI [withdrawing her hand – has the creeps]: Thank you, Doctor.

Lori sits across a table from Joyce. Decker sits against the wall.

> JOYCE: Miss Winston, are you sure you wouldn't rather postpone . . .
> LORI: No. Let's get it over with.

Joyce turns on a tape recorder on the table.

> JOYCE [starting at the beginning]: What was your relationship with Aaron Boone?
> LORI [pause]: We were lovers.

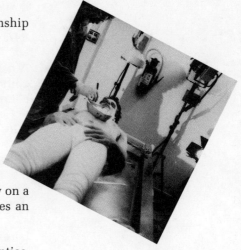

We move in on the revolving reels of the tape recorder.

> JOYCE: How long had you known Aaron Boone?
> LORI: Two months.

80. **INT.**   AUTOPSY ROOM   NIGHT

Burton and the attendant, instruments laid out, Boone's body on a brightly lit steel table, ready for the autopsy. Burton activates an overhead microphone.

> BURTON: Deceased is a white Caucasian male, late twenties. Suspected cause of death, multiple gunshot wounds to the thoracic cavity and extremities.

The attendant lifts up Boone's jacket. Light streams through many bullet holes.

> ASSISTANT: Jesus. They weren't takin' any chances.

Burton picks up a small digging tool and zeroes in on one of the chest wounds.

BURTON: Wound number one: entered between the fourth and fifth left ribs, impacted the lower rib, lodging in ligaments adjacent to the left lung . . .

He digs.

81. **INT.**   INTERVIEW ROOM   NIGHT

JOYCE: So he never gave any indication . . .
LORI: No . . .
JOYCE: Surely there must have been something . . .
LORI [firm, angry]: Look, you can say whatever you want to about him. I don't believe it. He never raised a hand to me, he never harmed anyone in his life.

A strained silence. Decker drums his fingers on his briefcase.

DECKER: Miss Winston, everyone has their secret faces . . .
LORI: Drop dead.

Annoyed at Decker, Joyce turns off the tape recorder.

JOYCE: We'll continue this some other time.

Lori stands and heads for the door.

82. **INT.**   AUTOPSY ROOM   NIGHT

A pair of callipers drop a distended bullet into a steel bowl, containing at least ten other similarly maimed bullets. Fatigued with effort, Burton wipes his forehead, turns off the microphone.

BURTON: Coffee break.

The attendant turns off the bright overheads, he and Burton move into an adjoining lounge.

83. **INT.**   MORGUE ENTRY WAY   NIGHT

Lori is putting on her coat. A contrite Decker approaches her.

DECKER: Miss Winston, I hope you didn't misinterpret what I said. Boone meant a great deal to me . . .
LORI: Where did he die? [pause] What was the name of the town?
DECKER: A place called Midian.

84. SCENE DELETED

85. **INT.**   AUTOPSY ROOM   NIGHT

The bowl wobbles on the ground. The bullets roll off in different directions. Sound of glass breaking.

86. **INT.**   MORGUE ENTRY WAY   NIGHT

Hearing the breaking glass, Lori and Decker turn back towards the autopsy room.

   LORI: Boone?

She runs towards the sound, Decker follows.

87. **EXT.**   MORGUE   NIGHT

In slow motion, a large first-floor window shatters out towards us.

88. **INT.**   AUTOPSY ROOM   NIGHT

As Lori, then Decker enter, moments after Burton, Joyce and the attendant. The autopsy table is empty.

   BURTON: Someone's taken him . . .
   DECKER: My God . . .
   ATTENDANT [looking around]: Where's his coat?

89. **EXT.**   MORGUE   NIGHT

Slow motion – distorting time, we see the rest of the shattering window and a dim figure crosses the moon.

                                        FADE OUT:
                                        FADE IN:

90. **INT.**   LORI'S APARTMENT   DAY

Lori hurriedly throws some belongings into a suitcase. We see some newspaper clippings beside the suitcase. A headline reads:

'SLASHER SUSPECT SLAIN'

Another features a map, showing the location of Midian.

91. **EXT.**   ROAD   DAY

Montage – Lori drives, at high speed, down the same roads Boone took previously.

92. **EXT.**   SHERE NECK ROAD   EVENING

At sunset, Lori enters the town, past a sign that reads:

'WELCOME TO SHERE NECK/ WELCOME BUFFALO DAYS RODEO'

93. **EXT.**   SHERE NECK MOTEL   EVENING

Lori pulls into the parking lot of the motel. A neon sign reads:

'THE SWEETGRASS INN'

Above it, the moon. From the motel itself, sounds of revelry.

94. **INT.**   MOTEL BAR   NIGHT

A wood-panelled, Western Frontier-themed bar. Country music. A banner welcomes rodeo participants. A number of rough types clustered at tables, many of them wearing baseball caps adorned with buffalo horns. Lori enters, looks around. A cowboy lassoes a waitress, ropes her in to general applause. Lori takes a seat at the bar and is approached by a bartender.

BARTENDER: What'll it be, darlin'?
LORI: A draft and some information please.
BARTENDER [taps a stein of draft]: There's the draft.
LORI [lays down a bill]: I'm looking for a town called Midian.
BARTENDER: You're not the first.
LORI: No?
BARTENDER: Had a bunch of TV news folks passin' through, since they nailed that baby-slasher up there.
LORI: Baby-slasher?
BARTENDER: Yeah, hell of a week for us. The rodeo this weekend. That scumbag gets blown away. I hear it took thirty slugs to bag that sucker. Just goes to show you, don't it? People love a spectacle.

Lori's hit with a burst of emotion. She doesn't want the bartender to see her cry.

　　LORI: Where's the bathroom?
　　BARTENDER: Right around the corner there, darlin'.

Lori rises, exits.

95.　**INT.**　　　MOTEL BATHROOM　　　DAY

Lori enters and leans on the sink as the grief hits her. She sobs. A stall door opens behind her: Sheryl, a girl in her early twenties, exits.
　　Lori pulls a tissue from her bag and tries to compose herself, standing back to allow Sheryl access to the mirror, where she studied herself before starting to tease her hair.

　　SHERYL: Which is it, hon', men or money? [Lori looks at her] It's usually one or the other, ain't it?
　　LORI: Oh . . . [a tiny smile] . . . A man.
　　SHERYL: Uh-huh. What'd he do, leave?
　　LORI: Not exactly.
　　SHERYL: Jesus, did he come back? That's even worse.

In spite of herself, Lori's brightened by the girl's good humor.

　　SHERYL [cont.]: Some loser takes a shine to ya, you could toss 'em in the river tied to a piano he'll come back faster than a dog with a bone. Thing is, why go to all this trouble to look so good if there's nobody to admire the end product, am I right?
　　LORI: Can't argue with that. [likes her, feeling lonely] Can I buy you a drink?
　　SHERYL: Hell, yes you can. Better than gettin' hit on by some damn buffalo.

　　　　　　　　　　　　　　　　　DISSOLVE TO:

96.　**INT.**　　　MOTEL BAR　　　NIGHT

Lori and Sheryl at the bar. Lori's nursing a beer. Sheryl's into her fourth Black Russian and is getting friendlier by the moment.

　　SHERYL [pause – just heard the story]: Lord. I have seen men go to great lengths to walk out on a girl. But, I must say, I have never heard tell of a fella doin' it while deceased.
　　LORI: They think some sick bastard's stole the body.
　　SHERYL: So you want to go check out the place in which he checked out?
　　LORI: Yeah. Guess it's a way to say goodbye, you know? He was always a mystery to me. I loved him . . . [she looks away]

SHERYL: Tell you what, Lori, why don't I drive up there to this Medium place with you tomorrow and keep you company?
LORI: You don't have to do that.
SHERYL: Yeah, but I'm goin' to and I don't want no argument from you.
LORI [smiles, grateful]: Okay. Thanks.
SHERYL: That's all right.
LORI [finishes her beer]: Guess I'll head up to my room.
SHERYL: You get some rest, sugar. I'm gonna stay down here and close this damn bar. Maybe one of these lunkheads'll win the lottery.

Lori smiles, squeezes her hand, exits the bar. Sheryl looks around, finishes her drink. The bartender sets another drink down in front of her.

BARTENDER: Courtesy of that gent in the suit at the end of the bar.

Sheryl looks down the bar, sees the man, seems impressed, waves.

SHERYL [low, to the bartender]: Isn't he just the picture of sophistication though?

96A. **EXT.**   NECROPOLIS   NIGHT

We Cut to a wide shot of the Necropolis by night. A shooting star falls.

Now we move in on one of the mausoleums, and from the ground below we hear a ritualistic chanting.

Once within the darkness of the mausoleum the camera slides down over the rock face into the depths of Midian. The volume of the chanting increases as we come close to its source.

96B.   **INT.**   MURAL CHAMBER

We come into the mural chamber, the camera passing down over the family tree of Naturals and Nightbreed and round to see Rachel and Kinski approaching and entering the door of the initiation chamber.

Cut to Narcisse and Boone, also approaching the chamber.

NARCISSE: You'll like this. No, really. It's just their way of welcoming you to the club.
BOONE: I'm not sure I want to be a member.
NARCISSE: You made your way back here for the same reasons I did. We belong here now. There's nowhere else on earth would take us in.

CUT TO:

96C. **INT.**   INITIATION CHAMBER

In the middle of the chamber is a kind of font, on which stands a bowl of Baphomet's blood, steaming and bubbling. Standing in front of it is Lylesburg. To his side Peloquin. Beside him, Rachel.

On Lylesburg's other side, Ohnaka. Standing around the walls as witnesses to the ceremony, are a variety of Breed.

Boone enters. The Breed all look his way. Boone sees Shuna Sassi.

> BOONE [to Narcisse in a whisper]: Who is she?
> NARCISSE: Shuna Sassi. Why?
> BOONE: I dreamt her.

Shuna leans towards Peloquin.

> SHUNA SASSI: I've dreamt him.

Narcisse nudges Boone forward.

> LYLESBURG: Who is your advocate?
> NARCISSE: I am.
> LYLESBURG: Have you tutored him in the Law?
> BOONE: Yes he has.
> LYLESBURG: Let the advocate answer.
> NARCISSE: Yes I have.
> LYLESBURG: You understand what you do, becoming one of us? With this night you turn your back on the Natural World. The life you lived will after this be as a dream.
> BOONE: I know.

Lylesburg takes the glove off his right hand. The flesh beneath is cauterized.

> LYLESBURG: The blood of the God tells all truths. It can harm as easily as heal. Are you prepared to be judged?
> BOONE: I'm ready.

Lylesburg nods, and puts his hand into the bowl of the blood. The blood bubbles around his wrist.

We cut to Peloquin and Shuna Sassi, who are watching Boone intently.

Boone's eyes are now on Lylesburg's smoking hand as it approaches Boone's chest, still marked by his wounds.

> LYLESBURG: Be judged.

He puts his hand on the bullet wounds. Boone stiffens. But there's no pain. When Lylesburg's hand is removed, the wounds have gone. There's a visible release of tension on the faces of all those watching.

> LYLESBURG: Aaron Boone, in the name of Baphomet, Lord of the tribes of the moon, I bid you welcome . . .

The camera moves out of the chamber, and towards the mural.

97. **INT.**   MOTEL BEDROOM   NIGHT

Lori lies awake in bed, staring at the ceiling. Outside, and next door, the noise of laughter and partying.

LORI [quietly, a tear in her eye]: I still love you, Boone . . .

DISSOLVE TO:

98. **INT.**   MOTEL BAR   DAY

Sheryl is sitting at the empty bar, obviously hung over. She is wearing dark glasses and a horned Buffalo Days hat. The bartender pours her an eye-opener.

BARTENDER: Hair of the dog.

Lori enters.

SHERYL: Hi.
LORI: How's your head?
SHERYL: My momma always used to say, 'Sheryl Ann, there's a man out walking around with your name on his mind, all you got to do is run into him.'
LORI: And he just happened to be checked in here at the cross-roads of the world.
SHERYL: Isn't that something? His name is Curtis, he is a banker, recently divorced and recently relocated in Edmonton, up for the rodeo and better yet, he thinks I am the Queen-bee's knees.
LORI: Sheryl, you sure you want to come along?
SHERYL: Wouldn't miss it. Besides, Curtis has to do business today, we've got an engagement for this evening and if I sit around all day with this head on I'm gonna feel like the hind end of a dog sled.
LORI: I'm glad for your company.
SHERYL: Now if we could just make a quick stop for some Alka-Seltzer.

DISSOLVE TO:

99. SCENE DELETED

100. **EXT.**   MIDIAN/**INT.**   LORI'S CAR   DAY

Lori's car comes to a stop near the edge of the reeds outside the Necropolis.

SHERYL: Jesus. Looks like the gold rush is over.

Lori parks the car. She gets out, looks around.

LORI [quiet – reflective]: Why? Why would Boone come here?
SHERYL: To get away from it all? [Lori gives her a look] Shut up,
Sheryl Ann. You go do what you have to do. I'll stay here and . . .
do somethin' else.

Lori nods and heads away down the street, leaving Sheryl beside
the car. She leans against the car, surveys the emptiness, without
enthusiasm.

SHERYL [cont.]: My luck, I'll end up buying some real estate.

101. **EXT.**   MIDIAN   DAY

Lori – as she leaves the reeds and sees the outer walls of the
Necropolis.

LORI: Good God . . .

102. **EXT.**   MIDIAN   DAY

Sheryl – wandering from the car into the reeds. She lights a cigarette, tunelessly humming to ward off the willies. She stops, shivers,
suddenly feeling very isolated. The atmosphere's got to her. She
starts back to the car.

She catches some movement out of the corner of her eye. Stops. Slowly walks away from the movement, fighting off panic. She turns a corner, and realizes she's lost in the reeds.

She hears movement behind her, turns, startled, then, oddly, she smiles.

SHERYL: Curtis . . . what are you doing here?

It's Decker, looking like a commuter, hair slicked back, wearing an overcoat, carrying his briefcase.

DECKER [big smile]: Hello, Sheryl Ann.

103. **EXT.** NECROPOLIS GATES DAY

Lori reaches the gates, slightly breathless. She pushes one of them open. The sun is hot and bright, transforming the Necropolis from the dark, dangerous place it was when Boone was here. Now, with its gothic tombs and burgeoning plant life, it's almost welcoming.

104. **EXT.** NECROPOLIS DAY

Lori wanders the walkways, enchanted by the splendor of the place. There are strange, bittersweet sights along the way: statues of dogs sleeping on their masters' graves; of mourning mothers; of children, sitting at their graves. And grotesque images too: gargoyles protecting the doorways of mausoleums; a tiger, roaring in stone. It is another world, solemn and silent.

Except . . . suddenly, the sound of an animal in pain. Lori stops and looks around. Her gaze comes to rest on a spreading laurel tree beneath which the shadows are pitch black. From here, the sobbing comes. She approaches. There is an animal beneath the tree, barely discernible. She can see its flanks panting, its head moving in pain.

LORI: Jesus . . .

It doesn't look like a recognizable species, an amalgam of wild cat and deer. She approaches. It raises its head, weakly. Its eyes are huge and black.

    LORI [cont.]: . . . It's okay, I won't hurt you . . . it's okay . . .

The creature shudders.

    LORI [cont.]: . . . What's happened to you? . . . Let me see.

She reaches beneath the branches and tentatively strokes the animal. It responds by dropping its head back on to the grass.

    LORI [cont.]: Oh God . . . you poor thing . . . don't die, please don't die.

She pushes beneath the tree, puts her arms beneath the creature and picks it up. It is heavy, a dead weight in her arms. She backs out from beneath the tree. As she steps back into the sun, the

creature snarls and starts to wither in her arms. She realizes what's causing it pain and steps back into shadow.

LORI [cont.]: You don't like the sun? Is that it?

The sound of sobbing, off to her left, draws her attention. One of the mausoleum doors is open, and a woman, Rachel, dressed in black, stands in the shadows, weeping. Lori's astonished.

LORI [cont.]: I'm sorry . . . is, is it yours?
RACHEL: Bring her. Bring her, please.

Shading the creature from the sun, Lori moves to the door and steps into the gloom.

105. **INT.**   MAUSOLEUM   DAY

The interior is marble, the air murky. Rachel, a fine-boned, pre-Raphaelite beauty in her thirties, moves back against the far wall, nursing a wounded arm.
   Lori looks down at the creature she's carrying, utterly limp in her arms.

LORI: . . . I'm afraid it's too late.
RACHEL: No . . . she can't die. Bring her to me, please.

Rachel reaches out. Lori's reluctant to move further into the darkness.

RACHEL: Hurry!

As Lori crosses the floor, she hears whispering from a stairway that leads down into the earth. She stops, frightened.

RACHEL: Pay no attention. Please, bring me my Babette.

As the creature is named it starts to move in Lori's arms. Not only move, but change. Its claws grab at Lori's breast as it writhes.

RACHEL [cont.]: Babette, no!
LORI: What's happening?
RACHEL: Don't look! Don't look!

But Lori can't help but look. Appalled, she tries to pull the transforming creature off her, but its hold is firm.

LORI: Jesus! Jesus!

With effort, she detaches the creature's claws from her, almost throwing it at Rachel, who cradles the changing creature in her arms.

RACHEL: Babette . . .

Lori leans against the wall, trying to wipe the sticky fluids the creature's exuded onto her hands. When she looks up she sees the creature in Rachel's arms has transformed into a pale, beautiful girl of seven or eight. Lori's dumbstruck.

LORI: What . . . what . . . what the . . . ?
RACHEL: She likes to play outside. I tell her: you mustn't play in the sun. The sun will hurt you. But she's just a child. She doesn't understand.

Lori looks back towards the open door, and the sun-drenched walkway outside. Then back at Babette.

LORI: This is too weird.
RACHEL [an urgent whisper]: You saved her. I owe you something . . . listen; I know why you came here.
LORI: You do?
RACHEL: You must go, this place is not for you. Midian is a home for the Nightbreed. Only for the Nightbreed.
LORI: Is Boone here? Did somebody bring him here?

A deep baritone voice rises up from the shadows of the stairwell.

LYLESBURG: Rachel . . . you have said too much already.

Lylesburg appears, a commanding, magisterial man with a vast grey beard and three slits on each cheek that look like gills. Loping along beside him, his fool, a muscular man with an innocently beautiful face: Ohnaka.

RACHEL: My Lylesburg, she brought me Babette, she saved her . . .
LYLESBURG: We know. But you cannot help her.
LORI [her spunk surfacing]: Look, I saved the child's life, don't I deserve something for that?
LYLESBURG: The child has no life to save. [he looks at her – sizes her up] But what she has is yours, if you want it. That's the Law. Do you want her?
LORI: No! I just want some answers.
LYLESBURG: You weren't meant to see this.
LORI: I kind of got that impression.
LYLESBURG: Then you also understand that to speak of this to anyone will bring dire consequences . . .
LORI: Hey, pal, don't threaten me.
LYLESBURG: Not for you. For us.

His words take the edge off Lori's anger. She notices that inscribed in the marble arch above the doorway are the words:

'WHAT'S BELOW REMAINS BELOW'

LYLESBURG [cont.]: What's below remains below. This is the Law.

Rachel is carrying Babette down the steps. Lylesburg turns to follow her.

LORI: Wait! Wait a minute! Boone, Aaron Boone, just tell me, is he here? You took him, you took his body, didn't you? Hey!

Lori crosses to the stairs. Lylesburg's disappeared down into the darkness.

LORI [cont.]: Talk to me, damn it, I have to know – come back!

105A. **INT.**   MAUSOLEUM STAIRWELL

Lori heads down the stairs.

LORI: Come back!

Lylesburg, Ohnaka, Rachel and Babette have gone, however. Lori continues her descent. There are sounds in the darkness below her. She stops, and looks back towards the top of the stairs. It's a long way off.

LORI [to herself]: How deep does this go?

She heads on down, turning a corner. In front of her, Peloquin. He starts towards her. She backs away, into a second creature, and starts up the stairs. As she does so a third creature swings down from the darkness above her head. She shrieks, and runs like hell.

PELOQUIN [calls after her]: Come back soon, y'hear?

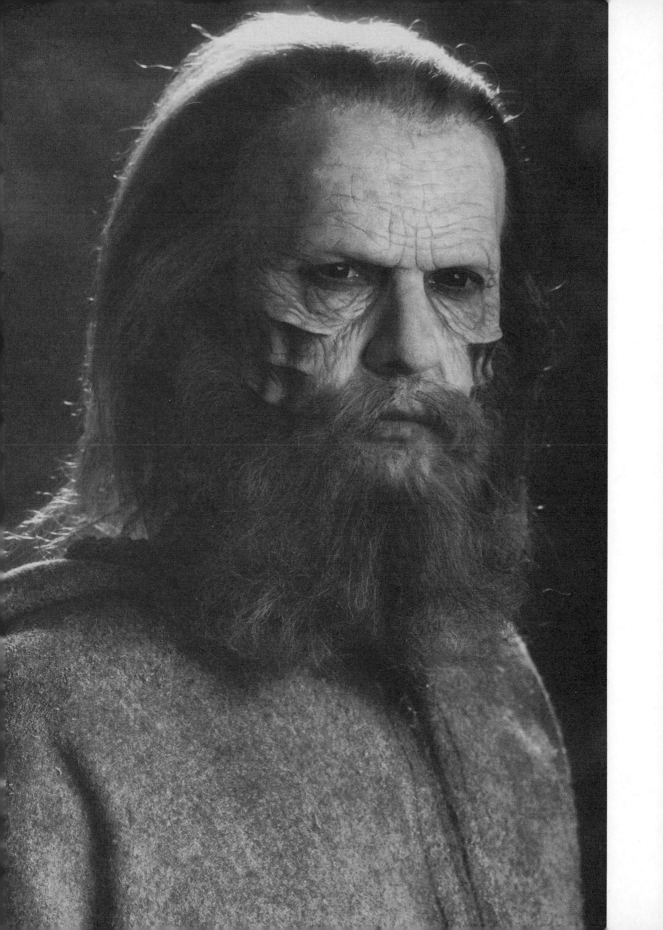

106.   **EXT.**   NECROPOLIS   DAY

Lori emerges, squinting against the blinding sun, trying to calm herself.

   LORI: Okay. Walk away, Lori. Don't panic. There's got to be a perfectly reasonable explanation. [can't sustain it] And hell if I know what it is.

She sprints back towards the gate.

                                        DISSOLVE TO:

107.   **EXT.**   MIDIAN   DAY

Out of breath, Lori reaches the car, parked where she left it. No sign of Sheryl.

LORI: Sheryl! Sheryl! Let's get the hell out of here! [no reply] Sheryl?

Lori looks around. Sees Sheryl's purse in the dirt near the reeds.

LORI [cont.]: Sheryl?

She moves towards the reeds. Picks up the purse. Peers inside the house. She hears a gurgling laugh from inside. It could be Sheryl.

LORI [cont.]: Sheryl, come on . . .

108. **EXT.**   REEDS   DAY

The undergrowth is dark and empty. Lori advances cautiously through the paths.

LORI: Sheryl, we have to go, uh, something's kind of come up and . . .

She sees a splash of blood on the reeds.

LORI [cont.]: Oh shit . . .

Something moves across our field of vision in the gloom behind her. She turns.

LORI [cont.]: Sheryl?

She turns back and follows the trail of blood around the corner. Lying on the floor is Sheryl. Mouth cut away. Tongue cut off.

LORI [cont.]: Jesus! God!

She turns to run, but Decker steps into her path. He wears a mask of repulsive simplicity: a linen face with two buttons for eyes and a zipper [open at present] for a mouth. In his hands are two large carving knives, both blood-stained.

DECKER: Let's get it over with, shall we?
LORI [mind racing, a survivor]: Take it easy, let's talk about this.
DECKER [advancing]: Don't try and reason with me, Lori. I'm a lunatic. You don't reason with lunatics.
LORI: How do you know my name?
DECKER: Good question. No reason why you shouldn't have an answer. [he pulls off the mask] Wish I had a camera. Oh, the look on your face.
LORI: Why? Why did you kill her?
DECKER: Why did I kill all the others? For the fun of it, of course. For pleasure. Everyone ought to have a hobby, don't you agree?

LORI: Boone was innocent.
DECKER: Is innocent, wherever he's hiding. After all the trouble I went to to find him a home for his guilt.
LORI: You sick motherfucker . . .
DECKER: Boone's alive, Lori. And your death is going to bring him out of hiding.

He comes at her suddenly, but his heel slides in Sheryl's blood. He falls in front of Lori, and stabs at her feet. She avoids the stab by an inch. He rises suddenly, throws one of his knives aside and grabs the blade Lori holds, with a glove which strikes sparks. It is chain mail. Lori lets go, propelling herself through the reeds.

109. SCENE DELETED

110. **INT.**   NECROPOLIS   LATE AFTERNOON

The light is diminishing behind the Necropolis walls. Lori's screams are distant. We track towards the gate as she runs down the hill.

LORI: Somebody help me!

She flings the gate open and enters. Decker emerges from the reeds behind her.

111. SCENE DELETED

111A. **INT.**   THE TEMPLE OF BAPHOMET

The temple is an impressive chamber, at the centre of which is a dais, ringed with representatives of the six failed saviours of Breed.

In the middle of the ring, a statue of Baphomet. There are benches along the walls. Sitting in them, reciting in soft, sibilant voices the Laws of Midian, are Breed.

Lylesburg, accompanied by Ohnaka, is also in the chamber, as is Boone, being held by the Breed.

BOONE: I have to help her!
LYLESBURG: You can't go.
BOONE: I'll kill him. No-one will ever know.
LYLESBURG: What's below remains below.
BOONE: I can't let her die.
LYLESBURG: When we took you in you made an oath to obey the Law.
BOONE: I won't listen to him butcher her. I love her.
LYLESBURG: She's a Natural. She couldn't love you back. Not now.
BOONE: Wrong!

He starts to struggle against his captors, fighting them off.

BOONE: You're wrong!

Throwing one back, and punching the other, Boone breaks for the door.

>   LYLESBURG: Boone! Boone!

Lylesburg's shout is ignored, as Boone heads up to the surface.

112.   **EXT.**   NECROPOLIS   LATE AFTERNOON

Lori runs down the walkways pursued by Decker, her breath coming in gasps, close to collapse.

>   LORI: Help me! Oh please, God, somebody.

113.   SCENE DELETED

114.   **EXT.**   NECROPOLIS   LATE AFTERNOON

Lori collapses. Decker reaches her and pulls on his mask.

>   DECKER: That's good. Be still. It's quicker that way.

He pulls a particularly nasty blade from his jacket interior and advances. She rises and tries to duck the cut. He strikes her with the back of his hand. She falls, striking her head on a tomb.

DECKER [cont.] [sudden fury]: I said, be still!

Lori is semi-conscious, blood running from her wounded head. Looking past Decker, she sees something . . .

LORI: Boone . . .

Decker laughs. Then he realizes she's reacting to the appearance of Boone, standing in the shadows behind him, in jeans and leather jacket.
Lori slips into unconsciousness.

DECKER: You? Here again?
BOONE: Isn't this where the dead are supposed to go?
DECKER: You're not dead.
BOONE [advancing]: You're wrong. We're both dead, Decker.
DECKER: I'm not Decker!
BOONE: No? Isn't that you, Dr Decker, hiding behind that child's mask?
DECKER: I'm not hiding . . .
BOONE [still advancing, taunting him]: Decker, Decker. Doctor Decker.

Enraged, Decker throws the knife; it buries in the middle of Boone's chest. Decker laughs, then stops, as Boone pulls the knife out and tosses it aside.

BOONE [cont.]: Blades are no better than bullets, Decker, don't you get it? I'm dead. The walking dead.
DECKER: That's not possible.

Decker turns to run, but Boone races to him, catches, turns him and pulls Decker closer, until they're nose to nose.

BOONE: Not just dead . . . changed. A monster. Want me to show you?
DECKER [whimpering]: No, please . . .
BOONE: Not your kind of monster. Not the soulless kind. I've got Midian in my veins.

He tears off the mask, uncovering Decker's sweaty, terrified face.

DECKER: Please, please, it's, it's not my fault, it's the mask, it makes me do things I don't want to . . . [Boone pulls him closer] Boone, it was the mask and they were going to find me, punish me, I needed a scapegoat . . .
BOONE: You chose the wrong man.
NARCISSE [V.O.]: Man? You call yourself a man?

Boone looks round; Narcisse is squatting on a tomb, his face a mass of scar tissue.

NARCISSE [cont.]: You're no more man than I am.
BOONE: Monster, then.
NARCISSE: That's more like it. [he jumps off the tomb, moves towards them] Well, go on, are you going to kill him or not? Only I want his balls. And his eyes. That is, if you don't want them.
BOONE: I'll pass.
NARCISSE: Remember me, Doctor? I was dying when you had your way with me. You made me tell my secrets when I was feeling particularly vulnerable. Now was that a nice thing for a doctor to do?
DECKER [to Boone, craven]: Oh God, Boone, don't let him touch me, anything, keep him off me, full confession . . . sweet Jesus, mercy, mercy, please, I'm begging you!

Narcisse raises his thumbs, still bearing their silver hooks.

  NARCISSE: Let's start with his eyes . . .
  BOONE: No!

Boone pushes Narcisse back, but as he does so Decker slips his
grasp. Boone roars and starts to twitch and stamp as Peloquin did
and we watch as . . .
  Boone transforms into something part man, part carnivore . . .
and gives chase.
  Decker nears the gate, but Boone is after him at great speed,
leaping over tombs like a high-jumper.

115. **EXT.**   NECROPOLIS   LATE AFTERNOON

Left behind, Narcisse turns his eyes upon the recumbent Lori.

  NARCISSE [filled with hunger, greatly consoled]: Well . . . you'll
  do.

As he advances on her, Lori's eyes flicker open. She screams.

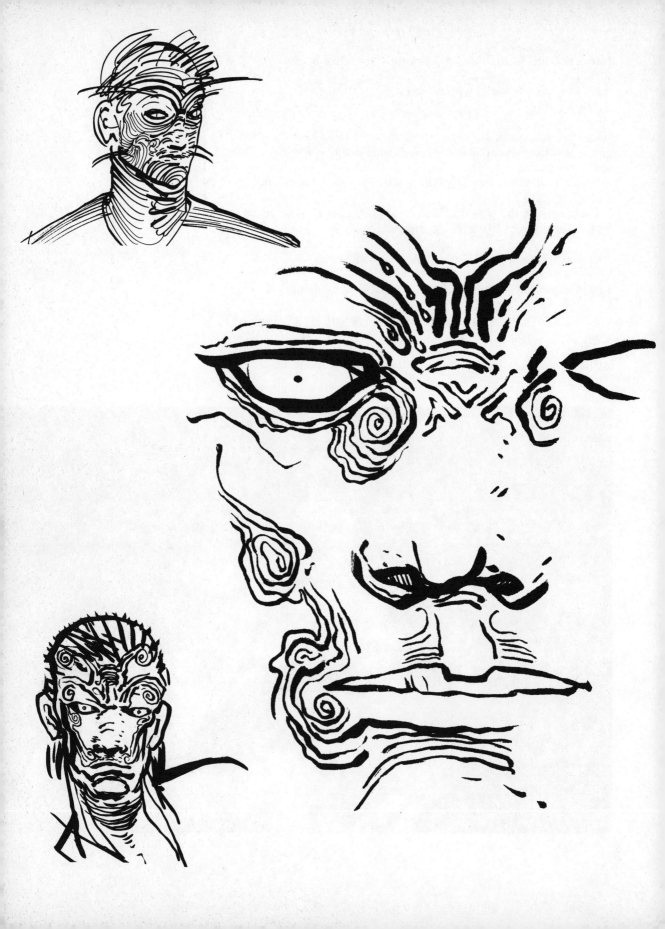

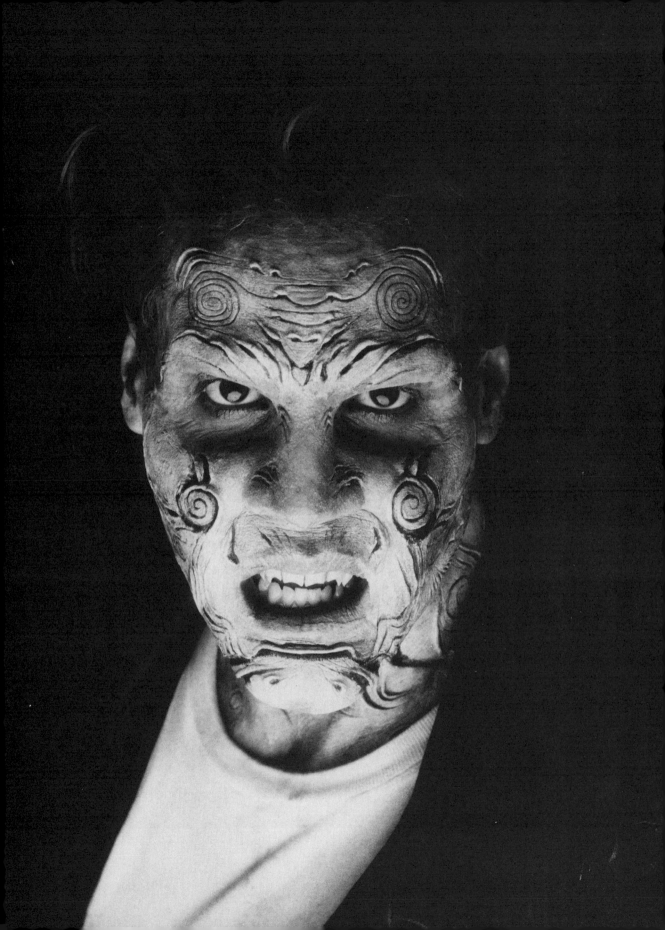

116. **EXT.**   NECROPOLIS   LATE AFTERNOON

Boone right on Decker's tail; he hears Lori's screams and stops.
Decker runs out through the gate. Boone starts back towards Lori.

                                                    INTERCUT:

117. **EXT.**   NECROPOLIS   LATE AFTERNOON

Lori struggling in Narcisse's arms. He tries to muffle her.
    Boone leaps tombs, nearing their location. He bounds into the
clearing, sees Lori unconscious in Narcisse's embrace.

    BOONE: Let her go!

Narcisse, all sheepish co-operation, gently lets her go onto the
ground.

    NARCISSE: Just . . . keeping her warm.

Boone is almost human now. He reaches Lori.

    NARCISSE [cont.]: I wouldn't have touched her.

Boone breathes in the last of his monstrous condition, and bends
to tenderly stroke Lori's face. Then, very lightly, he kisses her, and
gathers her in his arms.

                                                    FADE OUT:
                                                    FADE IN:

118. SCENE DELETED

118A. **INT.**   LYLESBURG'S CHAMBER

    BOONE: I had no choice.
    LYLESBURG: You've put us all in danger for your love of this
    woman.
    BOONE: Decker can't tell anyone. What's he going to say? That
    he tried to kill a girl and a dead man stopped him?
    LYLESBURG: He can still lead our enemies here. If he goes – if
    Midian's unearthed – you're responsible.
    BOONE: So let me make amends.
    LYLESBURG: Just take the girl and go on your way amongst the
    Naturals. That's the Law.
    BOONE: Who made this Law?
    LYLESBURG: Baphomet. The God in Obsidian. Who made
    Midian.
    BOONE: So maybe I should speak to this guy.
    LYLESBURG: Baphomet is a spirit in stone. He doesn't speak, or
    move. His wounds are too great . . .

BOONE: What are you afraid of?
LYLESBURG: What Baphomet made he has the power to un-
make. His blood is volatile. He mustn't be angered.
BOONE: Then I'll make nice.

119. SCENE DELETED

120. **INT.**   CORRIDOR BY LYLESBURG'S CHAMBER   NIGHT

Boone heads down the corridor. He slows as he passes an entrance
to one side chamber and looks in . . .
    Inside the chamber, a dog-faced man is working on a vast elabor-
ate mosaic mural that extends into shadow in both directions. He
looks up and locks eyes with Boone.
    Boone breaks off the contact and continues down the corridor.
    The dog-faced man turns back to his palette; a multi-coloured
collection of small tiles. He carefully selects a few, then turns to
the mosaic and we see . . .

121 **INT.**   MURAL CHAMBER   NIGHT

The mosaic mural. Prominent in what appears to be a panoramic
visual history of the Nightbreed race, is a heroic figure who closely
resembles . . . Boone. The dog-faced man applies the tiles he's
selected, filling in the irises of the Boone-figure's eyes.

122. **INT.**   RACHEL'S CHAMBER

Lori sits up.

    LORI: Boone . . .?

Her head aches. She winces. Babette goes to her aid.

BABETTE: Be still. It was a bad hurt he did us.

LORI: Us? What do you mean 'us'?

RACHEL [moving to them]: You held Babette while she transformed. She's made quite a bond with you.

BABETTE: I felt your hurt. I still feel it.

RACHEL: She even knew you were coming here. She saw it all, through your eyes.

BABETTE: And you can see through mine.

LORI [pause – she tries to read Rachel]: You're not kidding.

RACHEL: It's true.

Lori rises unsteadily to her feet. Babette takes her hand, but Rachel moves her away from Lori.

RACHEL [cont.]: She doesn't want you to touch her, sweet. She's afraid.

LORI: You got that right. One minute I'm about to get carved like a Christmas turkey, the next I'm . . . I'm . . . [a surfacing memory breaks her train] . . . God . . . it was Boone . . . Boone saved me.

RACHEL: Yes.

LORI: But he's dead, I saw him in the morgue . . .

RACHEL: You still don't understand, do you?

LORI: Wait a second, back up . . .

RACHEL: You're below now. With the Nightbreed. The last survivors of the great tribes.

LORI: Tribes of who? What?

RACHEL: We're shapeshifters; freaks; remains of races your species have almost driven to extinction.
LORI: So you're not immortal?
RACHEL: Far from it. The sun can kill some of us. Like Babette. She follows her father in that. Some of us could be shot down; others would survive that because they've got beyond death.
LORI: Horrible. It's all horrible.
RACHEL: To be able to fly? To be smoke, or a wolf; to know the night, and live in it forever? That's not so bad. You call us monsters, but when you dream, it's of flying and changing, and living without death. You envy us. And what you envy . . .
LORI [softly; understanding]: . . . We destroy . . .
RACHEL [to Babette]: Show her. Show her the past . . .

Babette touches Lori's arm.

BABETTE: Be with me.

The skulls in front of Lori fill her sight. We fly through one of the eye sockets into . . .

123. SCENE DELETED

123A. LORI/BABETTE'S VISION [TORTURE SEQUENCE]

Fade through from the skull chamber into grinning people running towards partially constructed bonfires . . . The people throw tinder onto the fires . . . We track off the fire-building to a wall, behind where frightened monsters hide . . . The shadow of a cross falls on them.

CUT TO:

126   NIGHTBREED

123B. LORI/BABETTE'S VISION [TORTURE SEQUENCE]

Inquisitors in black robes part to reveal the Head Inquisitor in purple robes . . .
 He reads the charges . . .

HEAD INQUISITOR: Thou shalt not suffer a monster to live . . .

CUT TO:

123C. LORI/BABETTE'S VISION [TORTURE SEQUENCE]

Frightened monsters pulled away from the wall.

CUT TO:

123D. LORI/BABETTE'S VISION [TORTURE SEQUENCE]

Inquisitors step aside to show torture scenes. We track through the tortures: racks, crucifixion, floggings, a hanging. The camera moves off gallows, past a wall to flags. We cut close on the flag which reads FREAK SHOW, track past the flag to a cage, containing freakish Breed.
 Well-dressed ordinary men and women applaud and laugh.
 One of the freaks is dragged from the cages. He looks back at the family he's left behind.
 The inquisitor reads their charges, as the bonfire awaits.

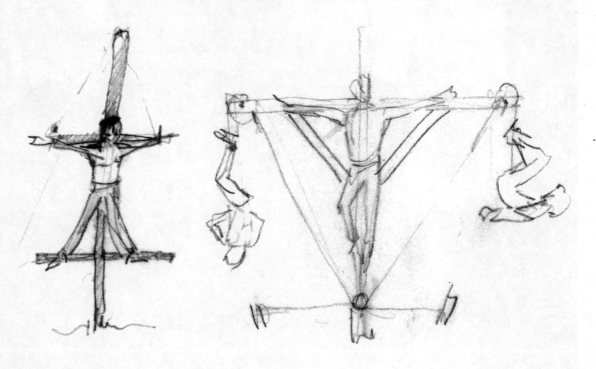

The Victim is thrown onto the bonfire. A tinder flares, and the inquisitors and audience light cigarettes and cigars from the tinder.

The bonfire then flares up.

An inquisitor lasciviously strokes the naked buttocks of a beautiful girl. She turns towards us in despair; we see her head is bestial.

124. **INT.**   RACHEL'S CHAMBER

Overwhelmed with horror, Lori opens her eyes, breaking her connection with Babette.

RACHEL: We are all that remain.
LORI: And . . . and you're saying . . . Boone's like you?
RACHEL: He is Nightbreed. Or he was, until he broke the Law.
LORI [moving towards the door]: No, no, that's not possible –
I've got to find him, there's been some kind of mistake . . .
BABETTE: Don't go . . .
LORI: But he didn't kill anybody, it wasn't him, he's innocent . . .
RACHEL: That no longer matters . . .
LORI: Where is he? Where'd he go?
RACHEL: Down to the Tabernacle, to Baphomet.
LORI: Who?
RACHEL: The Baptiser. Who made Midian. Who called us here and saved us from our enemies . . .
LORI: Take me there, I've got to find Boone . . .
RACHEL: It's forbidden.
LORI: We'll see about that.

125. **INT.**   EIGERMAN'S OFFICE

Decker is drinking coffee. A cop strides by. Joyce enters.

> JOYCE: Decker? This better be good.
> DECKER: I found Boone.
> JOYCE: Someone brought the corpse down here?
> DECKER: He's not dead.
> JOYCE: I saw him pumped full of bullets.
> DECKER: So did I. But he's alive. He killed again . . .
> JOYCE: In Shere Neck?
> DECKER: No, out at Midian.
> JOYCE: Why'd he go back there?

Eigerman enters.

> EIGERMAN: What are you doing in my office?
> KANE: This is Inspector Joyce. Calgary Police Department.
> EIGERMAN: We don't need any city boys on the case. Midian's under my jurisdiction.
> JOYCE: We can work together.
> EIGERMAN: No we don't. I'll bring him in myself. This is my town.
> DECKER: He's not alone anymore.
> JOYCE: What?
> EIGERMAN: Yeah. I heard that talk. That's nuthouse talk.
> JOYCE: Talk about what?
> DECKER: Midian's not empty. There's something breeding there. Below the cemetery.
> EIGERMAN: Bullshit.
> JOYCE [to Decker]: Do you believe that?
> DECKER: Yes I do. And if you don't stop them there's going to be more bloodshed. I promise.

126. SCENE DELETED

127. **INT.**   MIDIAN CENTRAL CORE

Lori finds herself in a cavernous space, lined with chambers connected by walkways and ladders, which don't look particularly secure. She moves out on to a walkway. It leads her into the central core of Midian, which offers a view of dizzying descent into the earth. She scans the scene, amazed by the sheer scale of the place.

> LORI: My God . . .

As she descends into the bowels of Midian, creatures in various doorways watch her with curiosity. One creature seems to have light running from wounds on its body. Another tumbles past her, a slow acrobat, defying gravity. She sees only a few of these but hears far more, chattering and murmuring in the shadows.

127A. **INT.**   MIDIAN CORE

As Lori moves through the chambers toward Peloquin we see the devil creature Lude feeding snakes to his pet, a horned, many-legged beast which squats on the floor. He gets up and goes to look at her. Leroy, a grinning grotesque, appears from the back of the chamber, snatches the snake from the maw of the pet, and comes to watch as well.

   LEROY [eating the snake]: There goes the neighbourhood.

128. SCENE DELETED

128A. **INT.**   MIDIAN CENTRAL CORE

Lori looks into a chamber. A dark, winged figure moves aside to reveal . . .
   A ceremony, with the bowls of white blood later seen in Bapho-met's chamber, is in progress.

128B. **INT.**   MIDIAN CENTRAL CORE

As Lori crosses the bridge something watches from the deep shadows . . . the tone darkens. She steps off the bridge and scorpions scuttle away. Lori is now a little nervous. She finds herself in a corner with several doors . . . Through one door she sees a man with a white T-shirt. She calls after him.

   LORI: Boone?

Lori enters through the door.

128C. **INT.**   MIDIAN CHAMBER

In a corner a ghastly meal is underway. The Boone figure is heading away through another door. Lori follows the figure, and the diners get up as if to attack. In the next chamber is a tangle of bright red glistening bodies with no heads . . . Lori glances round. The diners pursue her.

128D. **INT.**   MIDIAN CHAMBER

Up ahead of Lori is the Boone figure. She approaches it as it steps out of the shadows . . .
   It is not Boone!!
   She steps away . . .

128E. **INT.**   MIDIAN CHAMBER

The red beast is rising behind her. Lori turns and exits the chamber, flattening herself against the rock. She advances. Crouched in a

niche above where she's walking, we see a small lizard-like creature, Barabas, eating a dead rat.

128F. **INT.**   MIDIAN CHAMBER

Lori enters the final chamber, following the figure she thinks is
Boone.
    On the far side, crouching at a door, a figure.

LORI: Boone?

The figure turns. It's Peloquin.

PELOQUIN: No-one here of that name.

She turns. The Boone figure is in the doorway behind her. He has the face of a snake.

PELOQUIN: Told you!

He approaches Lori.

PELOQUIN: I know you. He talks about you. Lori.

He snatches a broach from her.

PELOQUIN: Nice. You're still a Natural. Want to join the family?
[he goes to bite her]
LORI: No!

Peloquin follows her to the door.

PELOQUIN [at door]: You will. Sooner or later you'll want to live forever.

He laughs maniacally, returning into his room.

129.   **INT.**   MIDIAN CENTRAL CORE

Lori continues her descent. As she nears the cavern floor, Lylesburg steps into her path, beside him his fool, Ohnaka.

LYLESBURG: You may go no further.
LORI: I want Boone!
LYLESBURG: You're not to blame, but you must understand: what Boone's done has put us in jeopardy . . .
LORI: No problem, you tell me where he is and we're outta here . . .
LYLESBURG: Boone has gone to Baphomet. He is beyond recall.

A low rumbling issues from somewhere deep inside the passage Lylesburg stands before. Underneath the rumble is an animal moaning with pain.

LORI: Where is he? He's down here isn't he? You want to stop me you're gonna have to kill me.

Impressed by her resolve, Lylesburg stands aside. She moves past him and heads down into the chamber, towards a distant light. Lylesburg gestures after her. Ohnaka nods and follows.

129A.   **INT.**   BERSERKERS' CORRIDOR ANTECHAMBER

Lori heads through a room which leads towards the Berserkers.

The reassuring sounds of the Core fade behind her. She slows her advance. Suddenly, Narcisse steps from the shadows.

> NARCISSE: Up and about already?
> LORI: Keep away from me.
> NARCISSE: I'm sorry about upstairs. I see a pretty face and I want to kiss it. [Lori moves on past] Don't go down there.
> LORI: Why not?
> NARCISSE [instant change of subject]: Don't you just love this place? Shangri-La on dope. I love it.
> LORI: What's that smell?
> NARCISSE [sniffs his armpits]: Not me. They keep the Berserkers down there. Mad bastards. They'll rip your head off and shit down your neck.
> LORI: Boone went this way, right?
> NARCISSE: And won't be coming back.
> LORI: I'll bring him.
> NARCISSE: You think love can raise the dead?
> LORI: He's not dead.
> NARCISSE: He's that and more. If you don't believe me, you wait 'til he gets to sniff a little blood. That'll bring out the beast in him. I'm telling you, don't go . . .
> LORI: I have to. Nothing makes any sense without him.
> NARCISSE: Sense? Who needs it?

Lori moves off down the corridor. Ohnaka follows her.

> NARCISSE [to Ohnaka]: Love those tattoos.

130. SCENE DELETED

131. SCENE DELETED

132. **INT.**   BERSERKERS' CORRIDOR

Lori starts down the corridor, the walls of which are cracked wide in places, the gaps covered with chains. From the other side she hears grunts and growls. Then, to her shock, one of the Berserkers' arms reaches up from a grille in the floor and snatches at her leg. She steps aside to avoid it, and another of the Berserkers' arms reaches through the mesh of chains, taking hold of her by the neck. It starts to choke her. She shouts for help.

Ohnaka, Lylesburg's fool, appears from down the corridor. He starts to rattle the chains further along the wall.

> OHNAKA: Hey, Ghost! Hey, Slaughter! Come and get me! Come and get me!

The arm around Lori's neck releases its hold, and we hear the sound of the creatures moving along the walls in Ohnaka's direction.

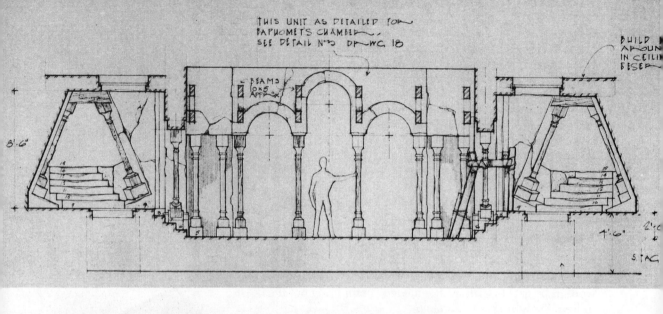

THIS UNIT AS DETAILED FOR
BAPHOMET'S CHAMBER
SEE DETAIL N° 3 DR-WG 18

BEAMS
10x5
APPROX

BUILD
AROUN
IN CEILI
BESER

8'-6"

4'-6"

2'-0

STAG

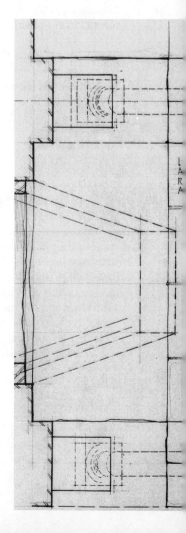

LARA

ORRIDOR

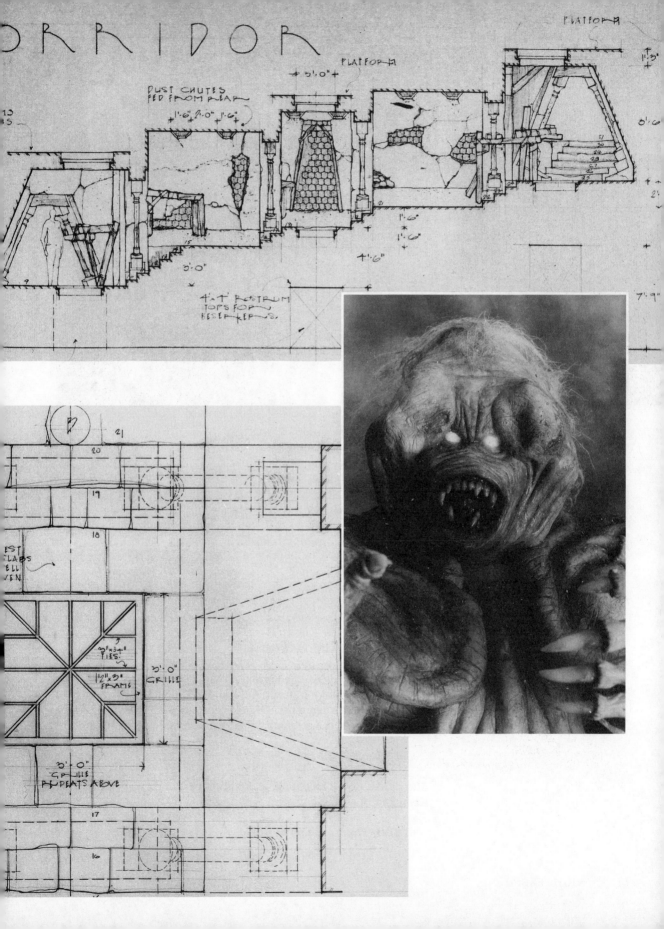

PLATFORM

PLATFORM

DUST CHUTES
FED FROM REAR

+ 5'.0" +

1'.6" 2'.0" 1'.6"

1'.3"

0'.6

2'

3'.0"

4'.6"

7'.9"

4 x 4 ROSTRUM
TOPS FOR
BEEFEATERS.

1'.6"

1'.6"

21

20

19

18

3"x 4"
TIES.

1½"x 3"
FRAME

3'.0"
GRILLE

3'.0"
GRILLE
REPEATS ABOVE

17

16

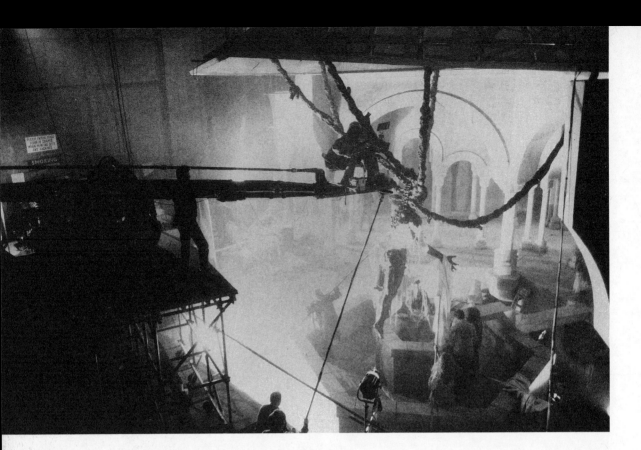

OHNAKA: Fat-asses!

Suddenly, arms reach for him through the chains. He steps away just in time.

OHNAKA: Missed!

He grins at Lori, proud of himself.

LORI: Where's Boone?
OHNAKA: This way!

He starts to lead her towards Baphomet's chamber.

133. **INT.**   OUTSIDE BAPHOMET'S CHAMBER

Ohnaka and Lori reach the next to last chamber; a roaring from below, down a slope in front of them, walls vibrating with the din from Baphomet's chamber. Ohnaka withdraws. Blindingly bright light, out of which Lori spots a figure climbing towards them.

LORI: Boone? Boone!

She moves down to Boone, scrambling up the slope towards her, drenched in sweat, half-mad with terror.

BOONE: Don't . . . don't look . . .

He reaches for her, then collapses. She starts down the slope to him. Dust falls from the roof, the din makes her reel. But she reaches him, starts to haul him to his feet. Then, she looks up and we get a glimpse of . . .

134. **INT.**   BAPHOMET'S CHAMBER

Out of the blinding light, and seemingly the source of it, a huge, black figure turns towards her, twelve feet high, severed limbs connected by sinews of hot, white energy and extruded spines, the face terrible, wise and beautiful.
   Lori's stunned, she averts her eyes. Boone collects himself enough to pull her away and they help each other frantically scrabble up the slope, out of the chamber.

135. **INT.**   OUTSIDE BAPHOMET'S CHAMBER

As Lori and Boone emerge, Ohnaka appears and beckons them to follow. Too exhausted and frightened to speak, Boone and Lori follow.

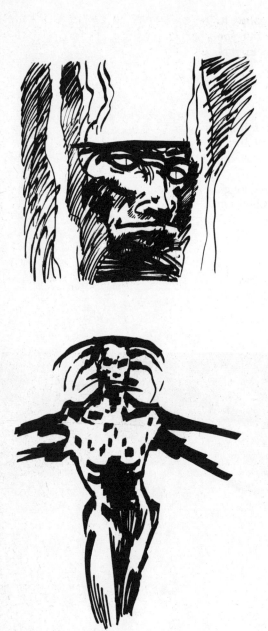
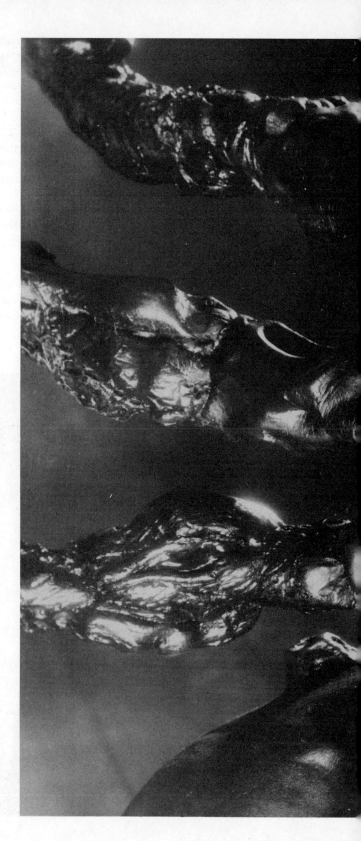

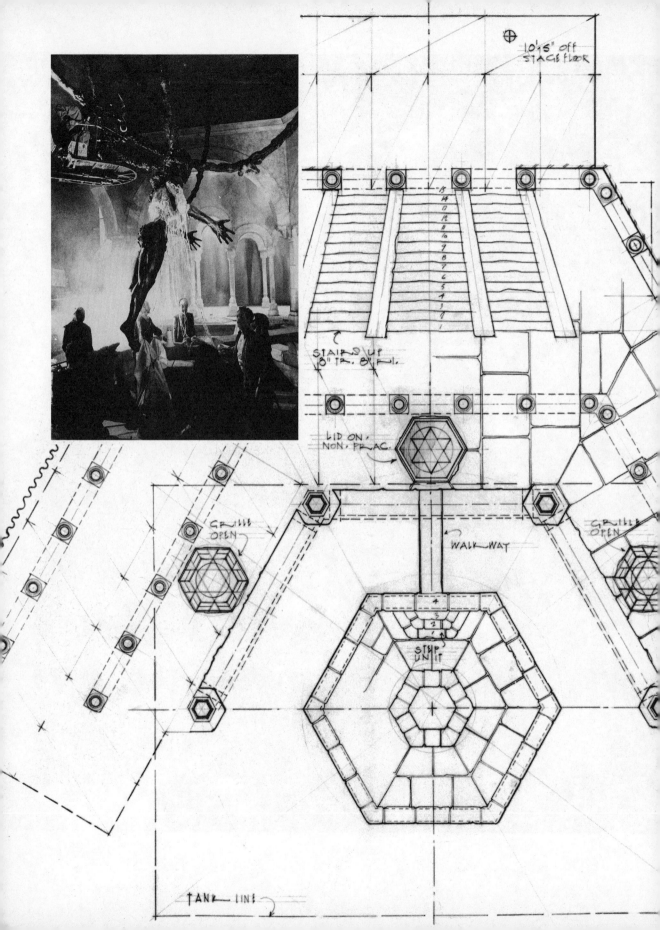

⊕ 10'5" OFF
STAGE FLOOR

STAIRS UP
6" TR. 8" RI.

LID ON.
NON· PRAC.

GRILLE
OPEN

GRILLE
OPEN

WALK WAY

STEP
UNIT

4
3
2
1

TANK LINE

ROOF PIECE
NOTE: COMPLETE FACETED
ROOF PIECE TO BE MADE
WITH FACILITY TO ROTATE AS REQD
FOR REVERSE SET UP.

1
DETAIL

WORK PLATFORM

7'0"

16'0"

CORNER CORBELS
TO SCULPT IN
POLYSTYRENE

5'+
TO

EDGE OF TOTS

136. **INT.**   MIDIAN CENTRAL CORE

Ominous rumblings urge them on, as Boone and Lori make a
stumbling ascent through the core, trailing Ohnaka's urgent lead,
watched from the doorways by a variety of creatures. We cut to the
ledge, and move to a chamber, where Peloquin and Shuna Sassi
are making love. Peloquin hears Lori urging Boone on as they
struggle across the bridge, and looks away from Shuna, out through
the door.

   PELOQUIN: Well, well . . .

He goes to the door.

   PELOQUIN [cont.]: Guess he couldn't take the heat.
   SHUNA SASSI: I dreamt him. He's strong.
   PELOQUIN: That's only because the bite was mine.
   SHUNA SASSI: No, don't you see? He's the one from the proph-
   esies. Cabal. The seventh saviour.
   PELOQUIN: So why's he leaving?

SHUNA SASSI: Everything has its purpose. Maybe he hasn't learned to hate his tribe enough. He'll be back.

Peloquin kisses her.

PELOQUIN: Why die waiting?

137. **EXT.**   NECROPOLIS DAY

The sun climbs over the horizon, sunlight penetrates the graveyard. A mausoleum door creaks open, Lori and Boone rush out into the open air. Lori tries to lead Boone away, he squints painfully against the early light.

BOONE: No, no, I belong here . . .
LORI [grabs him]: Bullshit! Boone, Boone, listen to me – you belong with me, that's why you lived, that's why we survived, because we belong together . . .

Ohnaka swings the door shut behind them. Boone sees Lori, as if for the first time. She takes his hand, presses it to her face, her breast.

LORI [cont.]: This is me. This is why I followed you, this is what we're living for.

His eyes clear. A part of him seems to return. He embraces her.

> BOONE: Lori . . .
> LORI: They don't need you. Nobody needs you but me. We'll go
> away, far away, where no-one will ever find us. I love you.

They hold each other.

138. **EXT.**   NECROPOLIS   DAY

LONG ANGLE:

Boone and Lori – two small figures, alone among the sepulchres.
They move towards the gate together.

FADE OUT:
FADE IN:

139. **EXT.**   SWEETGRASS INN   DAY

Empty streets. No activity. Lori's car pulls into the parking lot.

140. **INT.**   LORI'S CAR   DAY

Lori turns to Boone, slumped down in the passenger seat, out of
sight, wearing sunglasses.

> LORI: I'll get my stuff, I'll be back in two minutes . . .
> BOONE: Don't leave me alone.
> LORI: Boone . . .
> BOONE [fiercely]: No!
> LORI [calmly – trying to hide her alarm]: Okay. We'll go in to-
> gether.

She hands him the Buffalo Days hat and opens the door.

141. **EXT.**   PHONE BOOTH   DAY

From a phone booth across the street we see Lori and Boone move
towards the motel entrance. In foreground, a chain-mailed hand
picks up the phone and dials.

142. **INT.**   SWEETGRASS INN   DAY

Boone and Lori enter the corridor that leads to her room. Eerie
silence, save for a dog yapping somewhere. Boone stops. Alarmed,
she turns to him.

> LORI [whispers]: What's wrong?
> BOONE: Why is it so empty?
> LORI: They must be at the rodeo.

She hurries on, Boone follows, clearly disturbed. Lori unlocks her door, glancing back at Boone, who has taken off his sunglasses. There is something strange about the light in his eyes. A subtle wave of colour passes across his face.

    BOONE: I smell blood.
    LORI: What?
    BOONE: So much blood . . .

She swings the door open. We expect a horror. Nothing. An ordinary room.

    LORI: It's okay.

                                 INTERCUT:

143. **INT.**   MOTEL   LORI'S ROOM   DAY

Lori enters and quickly gathers her belongings together.
    Boone, sweating with terror, slides down the wall into a squatting position.
    As Lori packs, she looks down, sees a hole in the wall, the result of some massive violence from the other side. She cautiously leans down, peers through the hole and quickly retreats, hand over mouth, horrified by what she's seen.

    LORI: Boone?

Boone appears at the door.

    LORI [cont.]: Next door.

Boone goes next door and turns the handle.

144. SCENE DELETED

145. **INT.**   MOTEL   MURDER ROOM   DAY

Boone pushes the door open. Inside, a massacre: five dead card players, propped up around a poker table in a sick parody of a poker game tableau; throats slit, Buffalo Hats on their heads. Sitting in the middle of the table, a tall, elaborate house of cards.
    Boone moves into the middle of the room. On his face we can see the hunger he feels. Ripples of color begin to move over his features. He moves towards the corpses . . . as he does so, we hear a nearly deafening sound from outside . . . the vibrations knock over the house of cards and . . .

146. **EXT.**   SWEETGRASS INN   DAY

Into the empty street, a helicopter descends, discharging Lieutenant

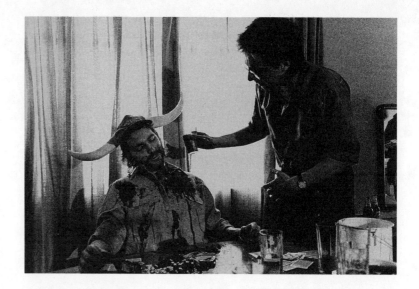

Joyce and a platoon of heavily armed Swat Team cops. Local police cars pour in.

Captain Eigerman climbs out of his cruiser to survey the siege. Decker introduces him to Joyce. Sharpshooters take up positions, training their weapons on the motel, as the Swat Team moves in.

147. **INT.** MOTEL CORRIDOR DAY

Lori moves to the door of the murder room. Boone is inside, his back to her.

> LORI: It was Decker . . . Decker did this . . .

In foreground, Boone's face begins to transform, which Lori can't see. She hears the cops outside.

> LORI [cont.]: Boone, we have to get out of here.
> BOONE: Stay away from me . . .
> LORI: Boone, what is it?
> BOONE: I don't want you to see . . .
> LORI: See what?
> BOONE: Get out! Do as I say!
> LORI: I won't leave you . . .

As she crosses towards him, he turns. His face is in mid-transformation.

148. **EXT.** SWEETGRASS INN DAY

Lori's scream echoes outside the motel. Joyce orders in the Swat Team. They charge, entering the motel.

149. **INT.** MOTEL CORRIDOR DAY

Lori backs out of the room in horror.

LORI: Oh my God . . . oh my God . . .

She hears cops charging up the stairs.

LORI [cont.]: Boone! They're coming!

INTERCUT:

150. **INT.**   MOTEL   MURDER ROOM   DAY

The transformed Boone covers his face, slams the room door shut
and moves towards the bodies.
    Lori hides at the end of the corridor as the Swat cops appear at
the far end.
    On his knees, in the middle of some frenzied action we can't
quite see, Boone stops and looks down at his blood-stained hands.

BOONE: No . . . No . . .

Out of sight, Lori watches the cops prepare to storm the room.

150A. **INT.**   MOTEL BATHROOM   DAY

Boone enters the bathroom with the sound of the Swat Team's entry to the motel on the track. He slams the door. There is blood on his face and hands. He goes to the sink and turns on the tap. Then he sees himself in the mirror, his transformed face is a shock. He looks at himself, appalled. Then a wave of nausea overtakes him. He throws up into the sink; a splash of blood and flesh he's just eaten. Wiping his mouth with the back of his hands he starts to breathe out his condition. His face transforms back to his normal state. He makes a sob of horror.

SWAT LEADER (V.O.): In here!

Boone looks towards the door, sinking down against the tiles as he does so. The door is flung open. We see him cowering as the Swat Team come for him.

151. SCENE DELETED

152. **EXT.**   SWEETGRASS INN   DAY

Under cover of the trees and cars around the motel, Lori hides in a place where she can view the front of the building.
　　She sees Eigerman talking with Joyce, Decker behind them. They look up as the Swat cops manhandle a hand-cuffed Boone out of the building. He has totally reverted to human form, the blood-stains seemingly a sure proof of guilt. Lori watches as he's thrown into a police car and driven off.

FADE OUT:
FADE IN:

153. **INT.**   SHERE NECK POLICE STATION   DAY

A clank of keys opening locks. A steel door swings open. Three cops rough-house Boone down the corridor, Eigerman right behind, passing other cells holding prisoners watching them go by. We hold on one, a young fundamentalist Baptist preacher, Reverend Ashberry. He has haunted, maniacally repressed eyes and the ragged look of a habitual drunk.

154. **INT.**   POLICE STATION CELL   DAY

Boone is thrown into the cell. Eigerman and the three cops, Labo-witz, Sergeant Pettine and Gibbs, all practised hard guys, enter the cell after him.

EIGERMAN: Fuckin' freak! Fuckin' cannibal! [to his men] Stand him up!

They haul Boone to his feet. Eigerman hits Boone with a wicked blackjack.

EIGERMAN [cont.]: You picked the wrong town, boy. We believe in real justice here. [a blow is delivered] They're gonna take you back to the city . . . [another blow] . . . but we're gonna leave you with something . . . [another blow] . . . to remember . . . [another] . . . us . . . by!

Boone sags to the ground, unconscious.

154A.   **INT.**   ASHBERRY'S CELL   DAY

As the sound of Boone being beaten up filters through the wall, Ashberry sits in his cell, Bible in hand. He flicks the pages over, attempting to distance himself from the violence he hears with study. He halts at a page with an illustration. It is something from Revelations: monsters and demons doing battle with angels. He puts the book down, and turns over his palm. It is a mass of tiny scars. He closes his hand into a white-knuckled fist, retreating into the shadows in the corner of his cell.

We cut back to his hand. Blood seeps between the fingers, as his nails dig into the meat of his palm.

155.   **INT.**   EIGERMAN'S OFFICE   DAY

Eigerman enters. Decker is standing looking at Eigerman's collection of photographs.

EIGERMAN: You still here?

DECKER: I'm going back to Midian with you.
EIGERMAN: I'm not going anywhere. We got press folks and photographers coming in from all over. Wouldn't be polite to keep 'em waiting.

Eigerman starts to exit again. Joyce is in the doorway.

EIGERMAN: Tell him. We got our man under lock and key.
DECKER: Don't trust him. He . . . he . . . changes. I've seen him.
EIGERMAN: I'll keep an eye out.
JOYCE: He was right about the motel.
EIGERMAN: So?
JOYCE: So maybe there *are* more of them . . .
EIGERMAN: Monsters?
JOYCE: Killers. A cult. I don't know.
EIGERMAN: You want to take some of the boys, take 'em Pettine?
PETTINE: Yes, Sir —
EIGERMAN: You, Tommy and Gibbs, take the Inspector out to the cemetery. Dig around. If you find anything with more than two eyes, holler. I got photographers wanting me . . .

He exits.

156. **INT.**   BOONE'S CELL   DAY

Badly beaten, Boone lies in the corner, stirring when he hears the door unlocked. Labowitz ushers in a middle-aged, small-town physician, Doctor Rose.

LABOWITZ: Doctor's here to examine you, freak. Just so nobody can say we laid a finger on you . . . [he winks at Rose] Looks okay to me, what do you think, Doc?

Boone painfully pulls himself upright. Looks up at Dr Rose, who slips on his stethoscope, listens to Boone's chest. He moves it, listens, moves it again, alarmed. He takes Boone's wrist, feels around. Boone stares at him. Dr Rose clears his throat, rises, moves to Labowitz at the door and speaks quietly.

DR ROSE: No pulse.
LABOWITZ: What's that?
DR ROSE: No . . . pulse.

157. **EXT.**   POLICE STATION   DAY

A crowd of journalists and on-lookers mill outside the station. We find Lori, following her through the crowd as she tries to get a view of the building.
    As she watches, Joyce and his three-cop escort climb into two police cars and drive off.

158. **INT.**   POLICE STATION   DAY

An impromptu press conference, with Eigerman centre stage, standing at a table laced with tape recorders and microphones. Behind him, a map of the town, with coloured pins and a black-board drawing of the Sweetgrass Inn, including a diagram of where the bodies were found. Eigerman adores the attention.

> EIGERMAN: Yes he may have had accomplices but I can't reveal the precise source of my information on that . . .
> 1ST REPORTER: Local source, Captain?
> EIGERMAN [a glance at Decker in the crowd]: Not so's you'd notice.
> 2ND REPORTER: Has Boone made a confession?
> EIGERMAN: We found him with a piece of human flesh in his mouth. How's that for guilty?

Cameras flash furiously. We see Labowitz leading Dr Rose through the crowd to the podium. Labowitz reaches Eigerman and whispers in his ear. Eigerman makes him repeat it. His brow knits in puzzlement. He turns to the press and smiles.

EIGERMAN [cont.]: 'Scuse me, folks, won't be a second.

Eigerman points a beckoning finger at Decker, who follows him into his office, along with Labowitz and Dr Rose.

159. **INT.**   EIGERMAN'S OFFICE   DAY

Eigerman closes the door and turns to Decker.

EIGERMAN: Just exactly how many bullets did they put into this geek up at Midian?
DECKER: Why?
DR ROSE [severely shaken]: Half of them are still in him. In fact, he's riddled with them.
DECKER: As I told you, these aren't ordinary people. You're saying he should be dead?
DR ROSE: No, I'm saying he is dead.
DECKER: When?
EIGERMAN: Not lying down dead, friend. Walkin' around in my fucking cell dead. Now what about that?

Decker's shaken. He grips his briefcase tightly.

160. **INT.**   BOONE'S CELL   DAY

Boone sits in his cell, head down, expression masked, eyes moving restlessly.

160A. **INT.**   ASHBERRY'S CELL   DAY

Ashberry is sitting half in shadow and half in light. His eyes carry the half-buried mania that we'll see erupt later on. He puts his head against the wall and speaks softly to Boone, his tone intensifying as his feelings take stronger hold.

> ASHBERRY: Can you hear me? They'll find a way to kill you, you know that? Can't fight the darkness. Not when it's inside you. Are you listening? You're an abomination, Boone. You have to die. There's lots of ways. I've read about them. Seen them when I sleep. Horrible. HEAR ME?

He suddenly slams his bloody hand against the wall.

> ASHBERRY: Have you got a God, Boone? Any God'll do. I had one, but . . . he doesn't listen any more. I ask him to take the dreams away but they keep coming. Blood and fire. Like the end of the world . . .

We move from Ashberry's stricken face to the bloody mark his hand left in the wall. It vaguely resembles something we recognize: Baphomet's head.

                                                    FADE OUT:
                                                    FADE IN:

161. **EXT.**   SHERE NECK STREET   DAY

Lori emerges from a supermarket with food to eat. She walks into a small square, finds a seat and sits down to eat. As she reaches into the bag:

> BABETTE [V.O.]: Lori?

She looks round. The voice sounded real. No sign of Babette.

> BABETTE [V.O. – cont.]: Lori . . . close your eyes.
> LORI [frightened]: Where are you?
> BABETTE [V.O.]: Please, do as I say.

Lori closes her eyes.

162. **INT.**   SKULL CHAMBER   CENTRE CORE

Lori and Babette's P.O.V. – darkness.

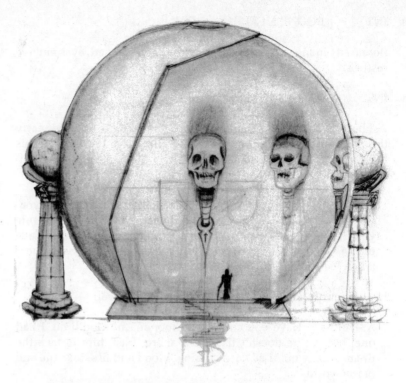

BABETTE [V.O.]: Be with me . . . be with me . . .

Dim light. We're in the Midian skull chamber, seeing it through Babette's eyes. Their voices merge into one.

LORI/BABETTE [V.O.]: . . . where am I? What's happening to me?

Rachel steps into view, and looks directly down at the camera.

RACHEL: What is it, child?

163. **EXT.**   SHERE NECK STREET   DAY

Lori's eyes spring open. She's terrified.

BABETTE [V.O.]: Lori! Come back!

Lori closes her eyes again and we click back into . . .

164. **EXT.**   SHERE NECK STREET   DAY

Lori and Babette's P.O.V. – we see Babette's view of Rachel.

LORI/BABETTE [V.O.]: Is this real?
RACHEL [whispers]: What are you talking about? Babette? [grips Babette] What have you done?
LORI/BABETTE [V.O.]: I've brought her, to see. She's in me.

Babette breaks away, Rachel tries to catch hold, Babette runs. P.O.V. camera veers around and down through the maze of Midian.

165. **EXT.**   SHERE NECK STREET   DAY

Eyes closed on the bench, Lori gasps as the journey snatches her up.

166. **INT.**   CENTRAL CORE

Lori and Babette's P.O.V. – Babette races over a rope-bridge. We see it all through her eyes, her hands coming occasionally into view. We head down a narrow tunnel and into a small chamber, which is Babette's hidehole. We scan the treasures she keeps there: a doll made of grasses; birds' skulls; pretty stones. We hear voices from above and we look up at a steel grille, facing out on the surface.

166A. **EXT.**   NECROPOLIS   DAY

Pushing closer to the grille we see . . . Joyce, Pettine, Tommy and Gibbs, wandering through the Necropolis, armed to the hilt. Only Joyce carries no weapon.

PETTINE: Christ, you could hide a fuckin' army in here.
TOMMY: What egg-zactly are we lookin' for, Sarge?
TOMMY [spits some tobacco juice on a tomb]: We're here to kick some major-league butt.
JOYCE [distrusts these throwbacks]: We're here to scout, not engage.
TOMMY: Well what if they engage us? What about that?
PETTINE: There's people down there, I can feel it.

Lori/Babette gasps, Pettine hears the sound and walks over to the grille.

TOMMY: Why don't we just shoot 'em in their graves? Save us diggin' new ones. [giggles – fires at one of the tombs]
JOYCE [angry]: Hold your fire!
PETTINE: We want prisoners, Tommy.

Pettine goes down on his haunches beside the grille, runs the muzzle of his gun along it. P.O.V. camera withdraws into the shadows. He shakes his head and . . .

167. **EXT.**   NECROPOLIS   DAY

We cut out of the P.O.V. as Pettine stands.

PETTINE: There's something down there all right.
JOYCE: If that's the case we'll call for back-up . . .

Pettine spots a movement in the shadows of a half-open mausoleum door. He catches Gibbs' eye, nods in the direction of the door. Gibbs gets the idea and starts to back towards the tomb.

PETTINE [a performance]: I don't know. Maybe we're just spooked. Hell, who'd live in a graveyard, anyway? [crossing towards Gibbs] What do you say, Lieutenant? Maybe we oughta just pack it in . . . head for home . . .

He and Gibbs rush the door of the tomb; there's a cry of surprise from inside.

168. **EXT.**   NECROPOLIS   DAY

Lori and Babette's P.O.V. – Camera glides back up to the grille in time to see Gibbs and Pettine drag Ohnaka out of darkness and into the sunlight where he lacks the strength to resist.

TOMMY: Well, lookee what we got here . . .

Tommy strikes Ohnaka with a rifle butt, knocking him to his knees.

169. **EXT.**   NECROPOLIS   DAY

As the cops circle around Ohnaka, he moans, puts his head down and covers his face with his hands.

GIBBS: Shit. Don't look so tough to me.
PETTINE: Want we should interrogate it, Lieutenant?
JOYCE [amazed]: Give it some room.

In the sunlight, Ohnaka's naked back begins to smoke and blister.

GIBBS: What the hell for?
JOYCE: God damn it! There's something wrong with him . . .

TOMMY [disgusted]: Shit . . .
PETTINE: What the fuck is this?

Gibbs, unfazed, steps up to Ohnaka and kicks the creature over.

GIBBS: We want answers, asshole!
JOYCE: Back off, Gibbs!

Gibbs ignores him, trying to drag Ohnaka's hands away from his face.

170. **EXT.**   NECROPOLIS   DAY

Lori and Babette's P.O.V. – Watching the knot of men around the defenceless Ohnaka.

LORI/BABETTE [V.O.]: The light . . .

171. **EXT.**   NECROPOLIS   DAY

Gibbs rifle-butts Ohnaka's hands, then pulls them away from his

face; the features are horribly disfigured, blood running from his eyes, scorched by the sun. Now even Gibbs tries to back away, but Ohnaka grabs hold of his shirt.

GIBBS: Shit! Shit! Get it off me! Tommy!
TOMMY: No way, man!

Pettine fires his piece at Ohnaka, hitting him in the belly and arm, but he still holds on, throwing back his head and howling. Smoke rises from his entire body, dust pours from his veins. The howl becomes a high-pitched whine and he explodes, in a burst of dust and black blood.

172.   **EXT.**   NECROPOLIS   DAY

Lori and Babette's P.O.V. – They see Ohnaka die.

173.   **EXT.**   SHERE NECK STREET   DAY

Lori opens her eyes, which are running with tears.

   LORI: Oh my God . . . oh my God . . .

She stands up, her hand to her mouth.

174.   **EXT.**   NECROPOLIS   DAY

Lori and Babette's P.O.V. – Babette's trembling hands hold onto the grille as she watches.

   BABETTE [V.O.]: Lori, don't leave, please don't leave me.

175.   **EXT.**   NECROPOLIS   DAY

The cops stare in disbelief at Ohnaka's dusty remains.

   PETTINE: Jesus . . . d'you see that fucker's face?
   JOYCE: It was the sun. The sun did it.
   GIBBS: Christ on a crutch . . .
   JOYCE: Man, that tears it, I'm calling the fuckin' chief.

Gibbs raises a trembling match to his cigarette as Tommy heads back to the cars.

   GIBBS: Couldn't have been just . . . just the sun . . .
   JOYCE: Believe it, shithead.
   PETTINE [grinning]: So if all it takes is the sun, we got the perfect weapon, right over our heads.
   JOYCE: Until it goes down.

Pettine's smile fades. Then a cry of alarm from the distance.

   TOMMY [V.O.]: Oh no! Shit! Pettine! Goddamn it!

The men rush to the gate.

176.   **EXT.**   NECROPOLIS GATES   DAY

The two police cars are on fire. The other cops reach them, Pettine reaches into the one less involved in flame and pulls out the radio microphone.

   JOYCE: Who did it, did you see anyone?

Tommy shakes his head. They all look up, hearing a distant car engine.

177.   **EXT./INT.**   BEAT-UP CAR   DAY

Wearing a hat and dark glasses, laughing, Narcisse drives this old clunker like a maniac, takes a large cigar out of his mouth.

He strikes a match off a thumb hook and lights up. In the back, protected from sunlight by shades on the windows, is Rachel.

178.   **INT.**   POLICE STATION TOILET   DAY

The door opens, a panicked Labowitz enters.

LABOWITZ: Chief, come quick . . .
EIGERMAN [from inside a stall]: This better be good . . .
LABOWITZ: Pettine's on the radio, they're under attack.
EIGERMAN: Hot damn, we got contact!

He bursts out of the stall, hitching his trousers.

179.   **INT.**   EIGERMAN'S OFFICE   DAY

Eigerman enters, takes the two-way receiver. Behind him, Decker, Labowitz and Kane enter the office.

EIGERMAN: Pettine, what's your situation.

INTERCUT:

180.   **EXT.**   NECROPOLIS
       INT.   EIGERMAN'S OFFICE   DAY

Pettine on the radio, as the others try to keep back the flames.

PETTINE [into radio]: The place is crawling with 'em . . . they torched our cars . . . fuckin' freaks! . . .

The transmission breaks up. Eigerman turns to the others in the room.

EIGERMAN [joyfully]: . . . Sound the call, boys, let the bells of freedom ring, we got to mobilize.

Decker affectionately runs his hand over his briefcase.

181.   **EXT.**   SHERE NECK   STREET   DAY

Lori moves down the street, blinking through tears.

BABETTE [V.O.]: I'm afraid . . .
LORI: I have to go, Babette, I have to get help. I'll be back, I promise. You hide somewhere.

The connection fades. Lori wipes the tears from her cheeks.

182. **INT.**   POLICE STATION   DAY

The crowd and journalists still hanging around; Eigerman throws
the door open.

 EIGERMAN: Listen up! We got officers under attack, I need
 volunteers for a posse! Y'all sign up with Officer Labowitz here!

He moves back towards the office, as Labowitz, clipboard in hand,
is besieged with offers.

183. **INT.**   EIGERMAN'S OFFICE   DAY

Decker is sitting with his briefcase open on his lap, gazing affectionately at the button head mask inside. He snaps the case shut as
Eigerman re-enters, followed by the silent Kane. Eigerman digs a
key out of his desk.

 EIGERMAN: If you're gonna make an omelette you have to break
 eggs, isn't that right, Professor?
 DECKER [doesn't follow]: Sorry?
 EIGERMAN: Christmas comes early this year.

184. **INT.**   POLICE STATION STORAGE ROOM   DAY

Eigerman leads Decker, Kane and another cop down into the bowels
of the station. He unlocks a door and switches on a light. Ware-
housed inside is a virtual arsenal in a number of packing crates
stencilled with a martial insignia and the name:

'SONS OF THE FREE:
SHERE NECK BRIGADE'

The crates are also stamped with their countries of origin: South
Africa and the Soviet Union.

    EIGERMAN: Ounce a' prevention is worth a pound a' cure. Save
for a rainy day, one day that day will come. Don't matter if it's
Commies, homos, freaks or Japs, we are ready. World class ord-
nance, Doc: the best private sector money can buy.

Kane, with a clipboard, goes over supplies with the other cop.

    KANE [over above – in his element]: Okay. We got your spankin'
new G3 thirty-odd-six Springfield semi-auto with roller-lock
action and retractable stock. For standard carbine firepower, you

can't beat this match-accurate Galil AR 7.62 NATO assault rifle and for the sportsman in the crowd we carry this handy, double-pump, Mossberg Persuader, sling swivels double extractors, which also comes in a light-weight single-barrel size for ladies and juniors –

DECKER: Marvelous, really, but –

KANE: Now over here we're talkin' Damascus, high-carbon Spetnatz shootin' knives, and for that tough up-close-and-personal work, you can always count on your razor-wire/fishing-line garotte when nuthin' else will do –

DECKER [over Kane]: Captain, have you considered the possibility that knives and bullets won't be adequate to the task?

EIGERMAN: Show him, Kane.

KANE [pulling off a shroud to unveil]: That's why we bought these cherry Israeli Army high-octane linear-field flame throwers.

EIGERMAN: Now I know what you're thinkin', Doc; maybe there's some sort'a spiritual angle to all this. Well, we got that covered, too.

185. **INT.**　　　POLICE STATION CELLS　　　NIGHT

A cell door swings open. Decker and Eigerman look in on the Baptist preacher, Reverend Ashberry.

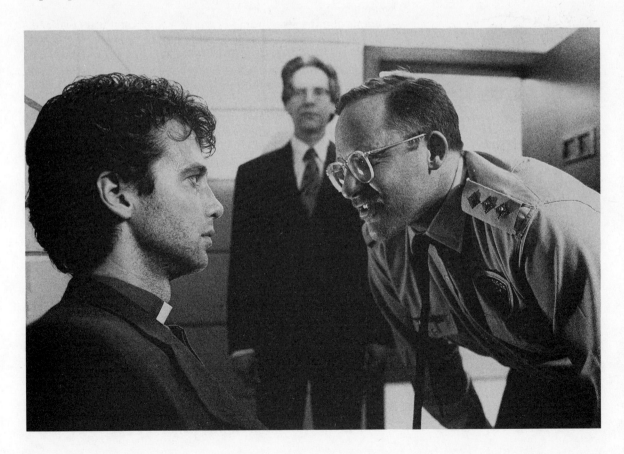

EIGERMAN: Reverend Ashberry, your services are required.

DECKER: He looks like a drunk.

EIGERMAN: He is; lost his way, poor bastard. [hauling Ashberry to his feet] You wouldn't wanna miss the Day of Judgment, now would you?

ASHBERRY [seems he's been waiting for this]: The Apocalypse? It's here?

EIGERMAN: They're warming up for it over in Midian. [leading him out] Padre, you get your pious butt over to church and load up on some Holy Water and crucifixes . . . we're goin' in there with God on our side.

DISSOLVE TO:

186. **EXT.** POLICE STATION DAY

Boone looks out the window of his cell as a large, unruly posse musters outside in a variety of vehicles. A mix of survivalist fanatics in *Sons of the Free*-labelled camouflage, Marlboro Men with six-shooters, red-neck bozos with their diesel-dyke mamas and heavily made-up bimbos out for a good time. The atmosphere is one of near carnival.

Accoutred for combat, Kane and some other cops distribute the weapons.

Boone slumps away from the window, his worst fears realized.

Reverend Ashberry arrives, lugging six full canteens and an arm-load of crucifixes. He loads into the back of an enclosed, high-tech camper with Eigerman and Decker. Eigerman blows an air-horn, claiming the crowd's attention.

EIGERMAN: You are all hereby deputized in the name of the law. Now let's kick some ass!

Eigerman's truck leads the caravan, which drives off, horns honking, war whoops and liquor-fuelled courage. As the dust clears now, left more or less alone, Lori looks at the police station.

A beat-up car squeals to a halt in front of her and the front door opens.

NARCISSE: Hey, chickie, want a ride?

LORI: No . . .

RACHEL: Please.

Lori sees Rachel and gets in the car.

187. **INT.** BEAT-UP CAR DAY

Narcisse drives around the block, smoking his cigar.

NARCISSE: We have to get Boone out, Midian needs him . . .

LORI: What could he do?

RACHEL: He went into Baphomet's chamber. He spoke with the Baptiser . . .

NARCISSE: And survived; nobody ever did that before.

RACHEL: Perhaps Baphomet told him something, something that could save Midian.

NARCISSE: Where they keeping him?

LORI: Inside somewhere. He'll be guarded.

RACHEL: He has powers of his own.

LORI: Tell me about it; what's happened to him?

NARCISSE: He was bitten by a Nightbreed, see, the taint's in his system . . .

RACHEL: Boone has been turned, he's one of us . . .

LORI: Okay. So what you're saying is, you're saying he's dead.

NARCISSE: Hey, some of my best friends are dead.

LORI [horrified]: . . . I'm going out of my mind.

NARCISSE [to Rachel]: See? I told you she'd take it well.

188. **EXT.**   HIGHWAY   DAY

The posse heads down the road, whoops and hollers emerging from the dust cloud it kicks up.

189. **INT.**   CAB OF EIGERMAN'S TRUCK   DAY

Eigerman cleans his silver-plate Magnum .45, Decker sits beside him holding his briefcase, across from Ashberry, who's frantically paging through an ancient Bible.

> EIGERMAN: Ever performed an exorcism, Father?
> ASHBERRY: No.
> EIGERMAN: Ever seen one?
> ASHBERRY: No.
> EIGERMAN: Well I'd start rehearsin' if I was you. [hands a gun towards Decker] Why don't you hang on to that, Doc?
> DECKER [a little prim]: Oh no, I wouldn't know how to use it . . .
> ASHBERRY [finds something in the book, reads]: Listen! 'So Moses spoke to the people, saying "Arm yourselves for war and let them go and take vengeance for the Lord on Midian . . ." and so they burned with fire all the cities where they dwelt and killed the kings of Midian, both man and beast!'
> EIGERMAN [with a wink]: Hey, how 'bout that, Doc? Sounds like we're on a crusade against the Devil himself.
> ASHBERRY [not terribly convincing]: I don't believe in the Devil.
> DECKER: Oh . . . you will.

Ashberry looks at Decker; no trace of irony in his expression. Ashberry sorts through the canteens, finds the one that doesn't have a white cross on it, opens it and knocks back two fingers of bourbon.

DISSOLVE TO:

190. **EXT.**   SHERE NECK POLICE STATION   DAY

The sun sinking low in the sky. The shadows are long.

191. **INT.**   POLICE STATION CELL CORRIDOR   DAY

The station is eerily quiet. Labowitz and an Irish cop, Connie Cormack, guard the cells. Two other cops patrol the end of the corridor. All heavily armed. Labowitz moves to the door of Boone's cell.

192. **INT.**   BOONE'S CELL   DAY

The spy-hole cover is open. Boone looks up.

> LABOWITZ [from other side of door]: Hey, freak-face, we found your pals. They're gonna fry, just like you. Give us a smile now.

Boone stares at the floor, depressed, defeated.

193. **INT.**   CELL CORRIDOR/OFFICE   DAY

Labowitz chuckles and closes the spy-hole. He walks back down to the coffee station near Eigerman's office, where Cormack is pouring two cups. He takes out a flask, spikes his mug and offers some to Labowitz.

  CORMACK: Little Irish in your joe, Constable Labowitz?
  LABOWITZ [a bad brogue]: Don't mind if I do, Constable Cormack.

There is a knock on the station door. They look at each other. Cormack picks up his gun and crosses to the door.

  CORMACK: Who's there?
  RACHEL [O.S.]: Help me, please.
  CORMACK: What's wrong?
  RACHEL [O.S.]: Accident. We need help.

Cormack decides to unbolt the door. On the step stands Rachel, shrouded in black veils. Only her eyes are visible. They fix Cormack.

  CORMACK: What's the problem, lady?

She drops the veil. The other half of her face has disappeared into smoke.

  CORMACK [cont.]: What the blazes?

Her costume falls to the ground. Her eyes dissolve. As smoke, Rachel blows into the station. Cormack fires through the smoke, yelling as he does so.

  LABOWITZ [running towards the cell]: Hold 'em, Connie!

194. **INT.**   CELL CORRIDOR   DAY

The two other cops hear the shot and run towards the station. Labowitz runs back in with them before they get there, slams and bolts the door.

  LABOWITZ [to the other cops]: Hold your ground! [yells through the door] Cormack? You all right?

195. **INT.**   POLICE STATION   DAY

Cormack turns back towards the door, sees Narcisse, screams and fires twice. Narcisse flips one of the bullets out of his chest with a thumb-nail, then leaps onto Cormack, who manages to shoot him-

self in the foot. Lori enters, slams the door and locks it. Narcisse squats over Cormack, holds his razor-nails under his chin.

NARCISSE: Where is he? Where's Boone?
CORMACK: Cell f-f-f-five . . . through the door . . .
NARCISSE [grins at Lori]: I love a coward.

196. **INT.**   CELL CORRIDOR DOOR   DAY

Labowitz and the other cops confidently prepare for a siege.

LABOWITZ [calling back to Boone]: Don't think you're getting sprung, freak. No way they get through that door; solid steel, armour-piercing shells wouldn't even make a dent . . .

Smoke seeps through the key-hole, and from beneath the connecting door.

LABOWITZ [cont.]: You hear me, freak? No fuckin' way!

The smoke from the key-hole begins to form into a face, which floats on a cord of smoke/flesh from the key-hole. The smoke from beneath the door forms into breasts and rib cage, in which a heart beats. Labowitz turns and sees it.

LABOWITZ [cont.]: Jesus Christ . . .

He empties his gun through the smoke; the two cops on the other side of the smoke are hit and go down.

An arm moves towards Labowitz; so does Rachel's face. Her beauty mesmerizes him. Her naked breasts, which float beneath the head, barely connected to it as yet, enchant him even more.

RACHEL: Come closer . . . I don't want to kill you . . .

Her hand presses Labowitz's rifle aside. Rachel's lips touch him. He doesn't resist, but once his mouth is sealed against hers he can't breathe. He tries to raise the rifle, but she dashes it from his hand. Then she snatches the keys from his belt and breaks the kiss. He falls to his knees, gasping. Her body completed and naked, Rachel unlocks the connecting door, then starts looking for Boone. Behind her, as Labowitz reaches for his gun, Narcisse's hand reaches in and grabs his throat.

NARCISSE: Naughty, naughty.

Labowitz looks up into Narcisse's scarred face and faints. Lori steps past Labowitz to the cell Rachel directs her towards.

RACHEL: We don't have much time.
LORI: I know.

Lori unlocks the door.

197. **INT.**   BOONE'S CELL   DAY

LORI [nervous]: Boone?
BOONE [wakes]: Stay away from me. I'll hurt you.
LORI: I don't think so.
BOONE: You know what I did in that room? I'm a goddamn cannibal. Stay away!
LORI: They're going to come for you.
BOONE: Let them. Let them find some way to kill me.
LORI: You can't die. Midian needs you.
BOONE: Midian's just a hole in the ground. It's full of things that should lie down and stay dead.
LORI: All right. If not for the Breed, then for me. You can't give up on us.
BOONE: You talk like you're one of them.
LORI: Maybe I wish I was. Some little part of me. [she puts her hand on his face] All I know is, I'm not afraid of you. I know I should be, but I'm not. I still want you, whatever you are. And I'm not going to leave you. If they come for you, then they'll have to kill me too.
BOONE: No!

LORI: So fight. For both of us. For all of us. I don't want to be ·
dust. I want us flesh and blood. Kiss me. I love you.

He kisses her. First tentatively, then with great passion.

198. **INT.**   CELL CORRIDOR   DAY

Narcisse knocks, calls through the door.

    NARCISSE: What the hell are you doing in there?

INTERCUT:

199. **INT.**   BOONE'S CELL   DAY

Fucking, is the answer. They are wound around each other: licking,
biting, gasping. Boone thrusts up into her.

    LORI: Yes . . . yes!
    NARCISSE [to himself]: Jesus. Bastard does better dead than I
did alive.

200. **INT.**   POLICE STATION   DAY

The connecting door flies open, a rejuvenated Boone and Lori move into the office where Narcisse and Rachel are waiting. Narcisse toys with the unconscious Cormack.

    RACHEL: Are we going?
    NARCISSE: About time.
    BOONE: Midian.
    NARCISSE: All right.
    BOONE: It's about time they saw the truth.

201. SCENE DELETED

202. **EXT.**   NECROPOLIS GATES   LATE AFTERNOON

Gibbs, Joyce, Tommy and Pettine wait outside the gates. Pettine paces. Joyce looks at his watch, moves over to Pettine and speaks quietly.

    JOYCE: How long until dark?
    PETTINE: Two hours. Two and a half. I told 'em to bring gasoline. We'll burn the bastards out.
    JOYCE: Has it occurred to you maybe we've got this all wrong? We could be destroying . . . I don't know, a whole new species.
    PETTINE: You saw that fucker below, Lieutenant, same as me. That damn thing was just too weird to live.
    JOYCE: Maybe they're just different.
    PETTINE: Isn't that enough reason?

Joyce stares at him. In background, Tommy starts to holler. Pettine calls.

PETTINE [cont.]: What is it?

Tommy is pointing frantically at a dust cloud in the distance.

203.   **EXT.**   ROAD TO MIDIAN   LATE AFTERNOON

A violent cut to the roar of engines as we track with the fast-moving posse. Eigerman stands up out of a skylight in the cab of his truck, eggs on the other vehicles with a rebel war cry.

   EIGERMAN: Yee-hah!

204.   **EXT.**   NECROPOLIS GATES   LATE AFTERNOON

As the caravan appears. Ecstasy. Tommy and Gibbs dance a jig together.

   GIBBS: It's the fuckin' cavalry!

The posse speeds down towards the Necropolis gates.

205.   **EXT.**   ROAD TO MIDIAN
      INT.   CAR   DUSK

Narcisse's beat-up car speeds down the highway towards Midian.

   BOONE: How much further?
   NARCISSE: A mile, maybe two . . .

We close in on Rachel, who stares ahead of her, as if in a trance.

   RACHEL: We're too late.
   NARCISSE: Hang on!

Steering hard, he veers the car off the road and into thick woods. Branches thrash against the windshield.

   NARCISSE [cont.]: This is a shortcut!

206.   **EXT.**   NECROPOLIS   DUSK

The posse is busily at work around the Necropolis, Eigerman and Kane supervising. Some are laying trails of gasoline through the pathways. Others are simply patrolling, guns in hand. There is an air of nervous anticipation.
  Ashberry comes round a tomb and we follow him down a walkway, staring in awe at the mausoleums and statuary.
  Looking at a particularly large tomb, Ashberry's eye is captivated by a large, fantastically rendered marble winged angel. He approaches it, reaches up to touch it. The angel, a monster, turns to look at him with sad, impassive gravity. Then we see its shadow

on Ashberry's face and hear the slow, thick beating of its wings as it flies off.

Ashberry's stunned. He fumbles the top of his bourbon canteen off, takes a long drink, then stops when he sees a load of dynamite taped to the side of the tomb. He follows the wire that leads off it to another dynamite pack on an adjacent tomb and then another. He's panicked.

207.   **EXT.**   NECROPOLIS   DUSK

Kane is escorting Eigerman and Pettine down a pathway, pointing out the posse's handiwork.

> KANE: . . . packets of plastique at every intersection, trip wires outside the biggest tombs, we figure those'll be the major escape routes . . .
> EIGERMAN: How much longer?
> KANE: Five minutes.
> EIGERMAN [into walkie-talkie]: Let's pull back to the perimeter before we lose the light. We've got movement underground; they're hearing it round the walls.
> ASHBERRY [approaching them from the side]: Captain!
> KANE: Jesus, not there, STOP. [Ashberry freezes] We got Claymores planted in the rosebushes, Reverend, cut your nuts off faster'n a hedge clipper.
> ASHBERRY: We've made a mistake, there are Angels here, a heavenly host . . .
> EIGERMAN: You're drunk, asshole.

Ashberry dumps the bourbon out of his canteen.

> ASHBERRY: No. Listen to me, it's wrong, it's sacrilege, this is holy ground . . .
> EIGERMAN: Get the hell up that hill, you pinhead.
> ASHBERRY: You brought me here because I'm a man of God.
> EIGERMAN: That's right; hang round here a couple more minutes, Padre, and you'll be sitting at his left hand. Now get your sorry ass out of the fuckin' way . . .

Eigerman backhands him. Ashberry falls. Eigerman, Kane, Pettine and the other cops begin to pull back.

Ashberry looks up, as he hears grindings and growls in the earth. Boone is lifting off the top of a nearby tomb. Ashberry is about to shoot when Narcisse grabs him around the throat, puts a finger to his lips and signals him to be quiet. Narcisse follows Boone into the tomb. The tomb-lid scrapes as it's pushed back into place from beneath. Ashberry starts to pray.

207A.   **INT.**   BELOW MIDIAN

Boone and Narcisse move through the panicking underground,

creatures fleeing in every direction. Boone sees Lylesburg, trying to keep the panic down, moves towards him.

> LYLESBURG: Stay down! Stay where you are, they're waiting for us above . . .
> BOONE [intercepting him]: No! if you stay here you'll be slaughtered . . .
> LYLESBURG: This is our home.
> BOONE: Not anymore . . .
> LYLESBURG: We belong here . . .
> BOONE: Listen to me, old man, the rules change; if you want to live it won't be here and it won't be by your laws . . .

Other creatures have stopped, watching the confrontation. Boone speaks to them as well.

> BOONE [cont.]: If you want to survive we've got to fight back, we can't hide anymore! [to Lylesburg] What's it gonna be?

Lylesburg slumps, acquiescing, unable to refuse Boone's assertions.

> BOONE [cont.] [to Narcisse]: Get the children above ground, find a hiding place . . . [to the others] Get ready to fight! [to Lylesburg] What about Baphomet? Can he be moved?
> LYLESBURG: Yes. It could be done.
> BOONE: It *must* be done. Brothers and sisters, it's time to fight!

207A. **INT.**   CHAMBERS

Leroy and Lude listen to Boone on the bridge.

LEROY: You hear what he said?
LUDE: What chance have we got? They're armed.
LEROY [opens jacket]: So am I.

Two one-eyed snakes, nesting in Leroy's belly, slide up from his innards and wrap around his neck.

LEROY: They call us monsters, remember? They're afraid of us. Let's give 'em reason.

LUDE: It's a long time since I spilled blood.
LEROY: You never lose the knack.

208. **EXT.**   HILL ABOVE THE NECROPOLIS   DUSK

From this high vantage point, Decker watches the preparations below through binoculars, with the glee of a pyromaniac at a firestorm. The sun is setting. He stares up at it, squinting into its brightness.

THE MASK [V.O.]: . . . I'm waiting . . . Philip? . . .

Decker looks towards the patrol car parked nearby. The front door is open. On the passenger seat sits his briefcase. Decker quickly crosses to the car.

DECKER: Be quiet.
THE MASK [V.O.]: Let me out, Philip. There's going to be bloodshed. I want to see.

Decker opens the briefcase. The mask and his knives are laid out inside.

THE MASK: Ah, that's better.
DECKER: We can't let anyone see us . . .
THE MASK: I want to be free!
JOYCE [V.O.]: Decker?

Decker swings round, slamming the case shut, as Joyce approaches.

DECKER: Lieutenant . . . [covering flawlessly] You gave me such a start.
JOYCE: Eigerman's invited you to watch from the command post.

DECKER: Oh, I don't think I'm up to it, really.

JOYCE: . . . I've got a bad feeling about this.

DECKER: Believe me, Lieutenant, whoever or whatever's living down there deserves what's coming.

JOYCE: Monsters, you mean?

DECKER: Unnatural, misbegotten creatures.

JOYCE: I don't know. The only monsters I've ever seen had a human face.

As Joyce looks down at the Necropolis, Decker sneaks an anxious side-long glance at his briefcase.

209. **INT.**   NECROPOLIS GATES   DUSK

The final explosives-layers exit, their backs covered by flame-thrower and machine-gun-carrying mob members. A distraught Ashberry is the last out.

Midian is now completely deserted. Dandelion seeds drift down the walkways, caught in shafts of sunlight.

210. **EXT.**   NECROPOLIS GATES/COMMAND POST   DUSK

Eigerman, Pettine and Kane, looking at their watches.

KANE [a pause – then]: . . . T-minus fifteen seconds . . . ten, nine, eight, seven, six, five, four, three, two, one . . .

EIGERMAN: Go.

Kane depresses the detonator. There are two large explosions, followed by several smaller ones. Part of the Necropolis wall is blasted out. Several members of the posse retreat. Eigerman pulls his pistol.

EIGERMAN [cont.]: You there, stand your ground! [fires a warn-ing shot] Stand your ground, damn you!

The defectors stop. Several more chain explosions in Necropolis.

211. SCENE DELETED

212. SCENE DELETED

213. **INT.**   BELOW MIDIAN

Narcisse is leading a group of child monsters, as the explosions bring earth plunging down from the ceiling. Babies cry. Monsters scream. We see several creatures howling in bestial terror.

Babette is separated from Narcisse's group by falling earth, nearly trampled in the chaos. She is picked up by the dog-faced man.

BABETTE: I want my mother.
MAN: We'll find her.

213A. **INT.**   PELOQUIN'S CHAMBER   NIGHT

Peloquin squats on the step overlooking the fire-pit, listening to the sound of invasion from above. There is a mixture of fear and rage on his face. In the darkness opposite, Kinski.

KINSKI: We began this.
PELOQUIN: I just wanted meat. I didn't know he was going to cause this.

KINSKI: There were prophesies. The seventh saviour.
PELOQUIN: I didn't believe the prophesies and I didn't obey the Law. You want to see me bleed for it? All right, I'll bleed.

He exits the chamber.

214. **EXT.**   NECROPOLIS GATES/COMMAND POST   NIGHT

Smoke billows over the walls. Eigerman moves closer to the gates, listening to the wild cries from inside. He grabs Ashberry by the collar.

EIGERMAN: That sound like a heavenly choir to you, Padre?
ASHBERRY: I have to see!

Ashberry shakes himself free and heads through the gates, into the Necropolis. Eigerman turns to the others, lights a cigar.

EIGERMAN: Pettine!
PETTINE: Chief?
EIGERMAN: We're moving in.
PETTINE [locks and loads his machine-gun]: Yes, sir! [turns – addresses the posse] We're movin' in!

Car engines are revved, headlights turned on, piercing the smoke.

215.   **EXT.**   NECROPOLIS   NIGHT

Ashberry wanders through the Necropolis as the Breed begin to emerge on every side.
    The air is full of sad, melodious sounds, like whale-song. Ghostly forms appear from the smoke and drift towards him.

ASHBERRY [in awe]: Dear Lord . . .

Some of the creatures brush him as they drift by: their strange beauty entrances him.

ASHBERRY: Dear Lord . . . Forgive me . . .

There are images here which have the flavour of Christian iconography. Mother and child. A man bleeding from his brow. A creature with a halo of smoke. He wanders on.

216.   SCENE DELETED

217.   **EXT.**   OUTSIDE NECROPOLIS   NIGHT

Decker watches impassively. Joyce moves towards the gate. As he reaches it an extraordinary creature appears.

JOYCE: My God.

It means no harm. Joyce steps aside and the creature moves off into the night.
    We cut back to Decker.

THE MASK [V.O.]: Don't deny me Philip . . .
DECKER: Soon. I promise.

Decker hears shouts to his flank, steps back, out of sight and sees Lori and Rachel emerge from a hiding place, Lori trying to restrain Rachel from going in.

RACHEL: Babette!
LORI: Rachel, no!

Rachel breaks away and runs towards the Necropolis. Lori is alone.

> THE MASK [V.O.]: Now, perfect, finish her. She's the only one who knows about us.
> DECKER: What about Boone?
> THE MASK [V.O.]: Boone's a monster. They all die tonight.
> DECKER [smiles]: All right.
> THE MASK [V.O.]: Quickly, Philip, we'll lose her.

The briefcase is opened. The light of distant fires flicker on the mask.

218. SCENE DELETED

218A. **INT.**   NECROPOLIS

Boone and Narcisse lead the column of Breed, children and babies up from underground into the Necropolis itself.

> BOONE: Hurry up.
> NARCISSE: Is this wise? Coming above ground?
> BOONE: If we stay below they'll slaughter us.
> NARCISSE: This is their territory.
> BOONE: No. The night's ours. Now get the rest of the children up here, I'm going to find a clear way through!

He heads away, leaving a frightened group of Breed and children.

218B. **EXT.**   GATES OF NECROPOLIS   NIGHT

Peloquin appears overground, scanning the destruction before racing off.

219. **EXT.**   GATES OF NECROPOLIS   NIGHT

Eigerman addresses the assembled posse.

> EIGERMAN: They're coming out, and they're armed, so watch yourselves. It's a fucking freak-show in there! We're not taking prisoners! It's us or them! Let's clean up!

The engines rev, and the posse charges the gates. The lead vehicle, driven by a manic, grinning Kane, rams the gates, and crashes through.

> KANE: Us or them! Us or them!

On the other side of the gates, Peloquin appears in Kane's headlights.

> KANE: Shit!

HEADLIGHTS HIT HUGE HOLE IN ROADWAY____

Peloquin jumps up into the air as the car careers towards him.

We see him somersault in the air. Kane hears him land on the car roof. We see Peloquin on the roof, bend over the windshield.

His face appears in front of a panicking Kane, the mouth suddenly opening grotesquely wide.

Kane slams the breaks on. Peloquin is thrown off.

KANE: Eat dirt, fucker!

Peloquin is thrown to the ground, his face caught in the blaze of headlights as Kane's vehicle revs and drives at him.

KANE [ecstatic]: Yeah!

His momentum carries the car towards the crater blown in the ground. Kane's pleasure turns to horror.

KANE: Oh shit! Shit!

He turns to swerve, but too late, the car heads over the edge.

Wounded, Peloquin crawls off.

219A. **INT.**   MIDIAN CORE

Dirt falls from the roof. Headlights appear.

219B. **INT.**   KANE'S CAR   NIGHT

The car slides into the earth. The guns stacked behind him fall forward.

KANE: Oh my Jesus!

219C. **INT.**   MIDIAN CORE

Kane's car drops through the roof of Midian, falling through the
core, breaking bridges as it falls. Breed are thrown off walkways to
their deaths. The car strikes the top of Baphomet's chamber and a
plume of fire, followed by several small explosions, marks Kane's
death.

219D. **INT.**   BAPHOMET'S CHAMBER

The explosions rock the chamber. Dirt falls. Baphomet looks towards the roof, with great sadness on his face.

219E. **INT.**   INITIATION CHAMBER

Boone enters the initiation chamber. Lylesburg is standing beside
the bowl of Baphomet's blood, which is bubbling furiously.

BOONE: What the hell are you doing down here? We need help!
LYLESBURG: This was intended.
BOONE: Fuck that! We're not going to lie down and die.
LYLESBURG: It's Baphomet's will. He's going to destroy the
Naturals, and us. Everything, in one last fire.
BOONE: How do you know?
LYLESBURG: Look for yourself.

He points to the bowl.

BOONE: It's going to blow?
LYLESBURG: Yes.
BOONE: He'll destroy his own people?

UNDER MIDIAN __ CAR FALLS IN __

LYLESBURG: Better it ends quickly. We can't escape them. We remind them of the darkness in themselves. They hate that.
BOONE: So did I. I learned better. We can make it out. But I need fighters.
LYLESBURG: We're not warriors . . .
BOONE: What about the Berserkers?
LYLESBURG: They're uncontrollable.
BOONE: All the better. Let them out. Don't just stand there! We're the tribes of the moon, remember?

Doubt and fear mingle in Lylesburg's look, but he finally nods his head.

LYLESBURG: I'll release the Berserkers.
BOONE: Be quick. We haven't got forever. Yet.

Lylesburg smiles. Boone leaves. The Drummer is at the door.

BOONE: You come with me. The rest of you get out of here.

He exits with the Drummer.

219F. **EXT.**   GATES   NIGHT

The posse enter in large numbers, firing to left and right. We see Breed shot down.

219G. **EXT.**   NECROPOLIS   NIGHT

Boone races to the entrance, to see Eigerman's posse moving towards the Necropolis. One of the posse has a flame thrower. He burns up the foliage. From Boone's P.O.V. we view the enemy: grinning sweating monsters. There's no way out in this direction.

219H. **EXT.**   GATES   NIGHT

Lori looks towards the conflagration.

LORI: Oh Jesus, Boone.

Behind her, we see a familiar, masked figure approaching: Decker. She doesn't hear him over the shouts and screams.

219I. **EXT.**   NECROPOLIS   NIGHT

One of the posse fires a rocket into a giant Breed who explodes. Boone reacts with horror at the destruction. When he turns back he sees Breed watching too, defenceless.

BOONE: Arm yourselves! Defend yourselves! You're not cattle, for Christ's sake. They don't have any right to kill you!

He races back the way he came, and pulls coffins from the walls, tearing their lids off with supernatural strength. He breaks the wood into clubs. The Breed watch him.

BOONE: Weapons! You need weapons or it's over!

One or two understand, and do as he's doing.

BOONE: All of you!

They do as he orders.

BOONE: Stop them getting in! They'll kill the children!

219J.   **EXT.**   GATES   NIGHT

Lori turns to see Decker appearing from the darkness. He attacks her, cutting her arm. She backs away before he can strike a second

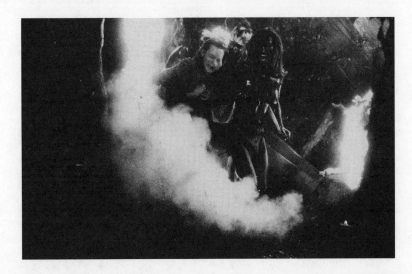

time, retreating towards the gates. Then she turns and walks through the reeds; Decker on her heels.

219K. **EXT.** NECROPOLIS NIGHT

The posse led by Pettine invade the entrances to the Necropolis, engaging in hand-to-hand combat with the Breed.

219L. **EXT.** NECROPOLIS NIGHT

Boone races through the Necropolis, finding that other posse members are breaking in from other sides.

BOONE: They're everywhere!

219M. **EXT.** NECROPOLIS NIGHT

The Nightbreed children hear the sound of slaughter approaching. One of the Breed with enormous, dark eyes, speaks.

LEOPARDO: We can't stay here.
NARCISSE: He told us to.
LEOPARDO: He can't help us. He's too late.

219N. **EXT.** NECROPOLIS NIGHT

We see the posse shooting Breed as they move towards the children. Several are entering doorways that lead underground.

219O. **INT.** MIDIAN CORE

Posse enter the core, firing at anything that moves.

219P. **INT.**   BERSERKERS' CORRIDOR

Lylesburg, his leg broken, is hobbling towards the Berserkers' chamber, as the sound of gunfire gets nearer.

219Q. **EXT.**   NECROPOLIS   NIGHT

Narcisse still keeps an increasingly panicked group of Breed and children from scattering.
Pettine and two bloodied, grinning posse appear through the smoke.

PETTINE: Look what we got here! A freak-show nursery school.

The group back away, but two more posse members appear, one with a flame-thrower, another with grenades.

PETTINE: Say goodnight.
BOONE [from above]: Goodnight.

Pettine looks up. Framed against the stars, Boone. He drops on Pettine breaking the man's neck. Then he and Narcisse lead the attack against the posse, dispatching them all.

NARCISSE: What way's safe?
BOONE: The west wall! But be quick! I'm going after Eigerman.

219R. **EXT.**   NECROPOLIS

Leroy and Lude hide around the corner of a mausoleum. Two posse members are beating a Breed up with their rifle butts. Leroy heads out to help.

LUDE: What's the plan?
LEROY: The usual. You take the big guy. [he yells to the Naturals] Hey!

They turn. Leroy raises his hands in surrender.

LEROY: I wouldn't do that if I were you.
1ST POSSE: Give me a good reason why not.
LEROY: I'll give you two!

The snakes emerge from his body.

1ST POSSE: Shit!

He raises his gun, but Lude flips over his head, landing behind him and in front of the 2nd posse member. Lude's eyes blaze.

LUDE: Pretty gun.

The 2nd posse member looks down at his hands. The gun is covered in snakes. He drops the gun. When he looks up Lude has gone. He turns again, backing off towards a monument. Lude is there, a living devil hidden amongst the carved variety. He takes hold of the man, turning him round and driving his horns into the man's neck. He staggers back, blood pouring from the opened wounds.

Leroy, meanwhile, draws the 1st into an embrace. The snakes strike. Poisoned, the man dies.

LEROY: Look at this mess.
LUDE: Just like the old days.

219S. **EXT.**   NECROPOLIS

Kane leads two cops through the mayhem, firing to right and left. He shoots a Breed against one of the mausoleums. Blood is spattered on his face.

KANE: Look at these bastards. Fucking freaks.

He wipes the blood from his face. Then he takes off his spectacles, and wipes the blood off them. As he does so 1st cop yelps.

1ST COP: Yow!
KANE: What?

1st cop pulls a quill from the back of his neck.

    1ST COP: Where the fuck did that come from?

Kane puts his spectacles back on, and sees Shuna Sassi in one of the mausoleums. She moves sexily in the shadows. Kane grins and starts to approach.

    2ND COP: Wait . . .
    KANE: It's just a girl . . .

1st cop is still rubbing the back of his neck. He is looking sick now.

    1ST COP: I don't . . . feel . . . so . . . good . . .

Kane pushes the mausoleum grille open, as the 1st cop kneels over, face down. The 2nd cop kneels to help him. Meanwhile, Kane has stepped into the mausoleum. Shuna is in the corner, her spines covered with the swaths of red cloth.

    KANE: It's OK, Baby.

He lowers his gun. Outside the 2nd cop turns the 1st over. He is frothing at the mouth, his face blotchy and sweating.

    2ND COP: Oh shit! Kane!

Inside again, Shuna drops her cloth and leaps at Kane. 2nd cop now approaches the mausoleum.

    2ND COP: Kane?

As he reaches the threshold, Kane staggers out, his body and face pierced in dozens of places with Shuna's spines. He reaches for 2nd cop.

    2ND COP: Keep away from me!

In panic, he fires at Kane, who falls to the ground. As the smoke clears a hand appears and strokes his cheek. He turns. It's Shuna. He screams, and falls to the ground at her feet, his arm covered in spines. He twitches, and dies. She drops her swath of red cloth over the faces of the three dead men.

SCENES 220–224 DELETED

225.   **EXT.**   NECROPOLIS GATES   NIGHT

Cut to Eigerman's leering, grinning face as he fires at Breed. Ashberry emerges from the shadows and grabs him.

ASHBERRY: Please, you've got to stop . . . [takes out a pistol –
points it) There's children down there, you're killing children!
EIGERMAN: Go ahead, faggot. [pauses contemptuously] You
haven't got the balls to pull the trigger.

Eigerman snatches the gun away and pistol-whips him to the
ground. Eigerman draws a bead on Ashberry's forehead.

EIGERMAN [cont.]: Lemme show you how it's done . . .

Nearby, Joyce sees them, draws his weapon, ready to fire at Eigerman when a shadow passes over him. He ducks, his expression
changing from horror to wonder.

ASHBERRY [eyes closed – hands clasped fervently]: Father, I am
heartily sorry for having offended thee . . .

EIGERMAN: Sorry, Padre. Nobody's listening . . . [prepares to shoot]
BOONE [V.O.]: I hear you.

Eigerman turns, looks and fires as Boone leaps at him. He roars, effortlessly picks Eigerman up and body-slams him against the wall of Midian.

BOONE [cont.] [to Ashberry]: Get up!
ASHBERRY: Don't kill me!
BOONE: Run, go on! We don't like priests here.

Ashberry pulls at his collar, tears it off, clings to Boone.

ASHBERRY: No, no, take me, I have to see.

Boone gets a sense of his commitment. He heads off. Ashberry follows. And, at a distance, so does Joyce.

226. **EXT.**   NECROPOLIS   NIGHT

Boone races through the walkways, Ashberry following. There is pitched hand-to-hand battle on every side. Nightbreed are prevailing in some; in others the mob repeats scenes from the history we witnessed earlier: Breed being beaten or burned to death, impaled on stakes. Boone assists some along the way, pulling off their assailants.

227. **EXT.**   NECROPOLIS GATES   NIGHT

Lori enters the Necropolis, running through the smoke. Decker follows.

   LORI: Boone! Boone!

228A. SCENE DELETED

229. **INT.**   BERSERKERS' CORRIDOR

Lylesburg has reached the door of the Berserkers' chamber. He puts the key in the lock. A shout stops him turning it. He looks towards a man with a laser-sight rifle.

   MAN: Yo!

The light from the rifle plays on Lylesburg's robes.

   MAN: Watch the pretty light.

It moves up towards Lylesburg's face, until it's centred on his forehead. The man fires, killing his victim. Lylesburg falls, hanging from the door by the key chain around his neck. His many eyes have opened. The man grins. Then hears a noise behind him. He turns to see the Ferreol Vees, creatures like Manta Rays that glide

through the air, appearing around the corner. They swoop towards him, separating. The middle one opens its mouth as it strikes his face. He is eclipsed. When the Vees pass on down the corridor, the man's face is a bloody wreck. He falls to the floor, just out of reach of the Berserkers, who roar their frustration.

230. **INT.**   MIDIAN CORE

Boone and Ashberry are on one of the walkways, which are swinging violently. Boone hears the Berserkers' roar, and heads towards the door that leads into their corridor, leaving Ashberry on the bridge, tears pouring down his face. Then he follows Boone. As he reaches the ledge he looks back to see a fabulous beast, the Mezzick-Muul, and its beautiful rider, Diadaria, appear. He watches, awestruck.

230A. **EXT.**   NECROPOLIS   NIGHT

Lori races through the smoke and horror of the Necropolis, as Decker follows.

231. **INT.**   BERSERKERS' CHAMBER

Boone reaches the door. Lylesburg is dead. Boone pulls the key from off Lylesburg's neck, and pulls the corpse aside. Then he turns the key in the lock. The door opens. A rush of filthy wind emerges from the chamber beyond. Then the Berserkers appear:

lethal brutes, all teeth, armour and muscle. One of them, Ghost, takes hold of Boone, and there's a beat when it seems certain to dispatch him.

Then a burst of light from Baphomet's chamber spills over them, and there's a roar from their unseen God. They let Boone go, and they're away. Boone looks towards the chamber, then heads back towards the surface.

SCENES 232–235 DELETED

236.   **EXT.**   NECROPOLIS   NIGHT

Tommy leads a line of five posse members who have cornered a number of wounded Breed against one of the walls. One of the creatures attempts to scramble away. Tommy guns him down. He turns to the other gunmen.

TOMMY: Watch this!

The two posse members prepare to kill the Breed. The ground around them begins to shudder, and a fist bursts out of the ground and grabs the leg of a posse member and drags him down.

Another fist then bursts out of the ground.

Then in silhouette the Berserkers climb out of the earth beside the posse. Two of the posse turn, and fire at the Berserkers, who advance through the hail of the bullets, and quickly dispatch the two gunmen. Tommy has begun to fire at the feet of the cornered Breed, obliging them to dance.

TOMMY [laughs]: Dance, fuckers!

The display gets appreciative hoots and laughter from the three surviving posse members, who – like Tommy – are as yet unaware that the Berserkers are advancing on them. Tommy continues to fire at the ground around the Breed, as one by one his three companions are dispatched by the Berserkers. We close in on Tommy, whose face is suddenly spattered with blood. He stops firing. He looks round to find himself surrounded by Berserkers. The shadows fall over him. Their hands take hold of him.

We see the shadow of what they do to him on the walls: his body is torn apart.

We cut to the Berserkers. Ghost has Tommy's gun, with the hand still attached. He tosses it aside, roaring like King Kong. The wounded Breed hurry away as the Berserkers head off in search of new mischief.

237.   **EXT.**   NECROPOLIS   NEAR THE GATES   NIGHT

With the tide turning inside the Necropolis, a disorganized retreat is underway. Eigerman is at the gate watching the remains of his 'army' staggering away. Joyce is watching the scene.

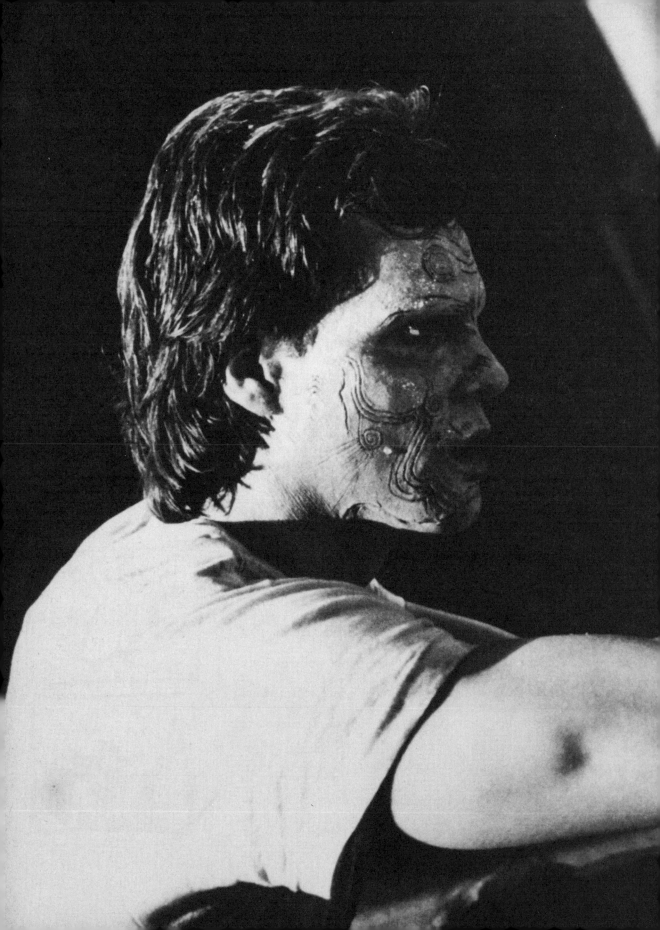

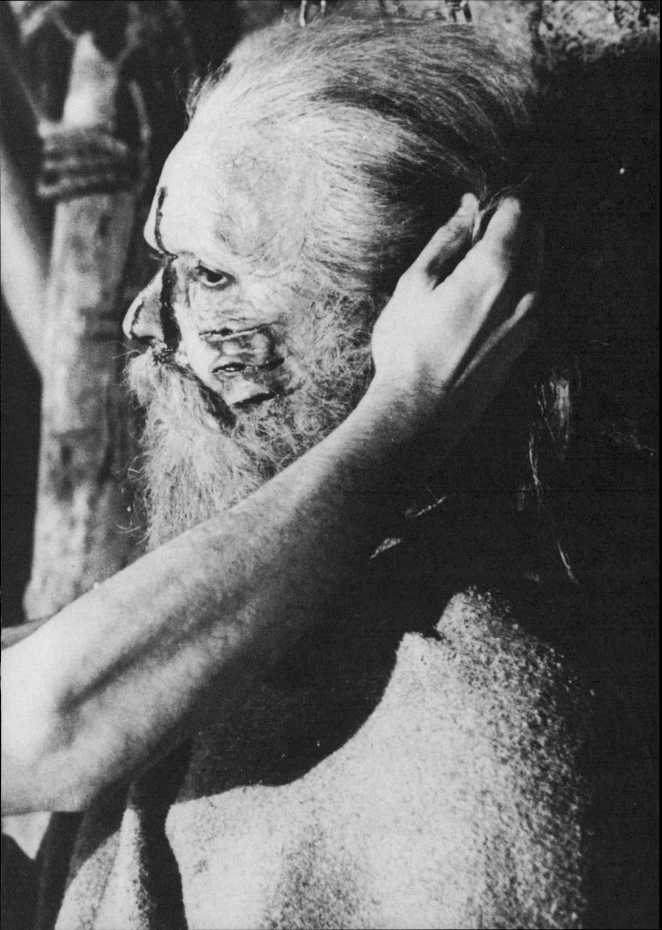

EIGERMAN: Stand your ground! Stand your ground! They've got to come this way. We can mow 'em down.

He climbs up on a vehicle which is parked at the gates. In the driving seat is Gibbs. Beside him, a woman, her face smoke-stained, her expression near catatonic.

EIGERMAN: Gibbs?
GIBBS: Sir?
EIGERMAN: Lights!

Gibbs switches the lights on, to pierce the smoke. Bad move. The illumination shows the Berserkers appearing. They approach the vehicle.

EIGERMAN: Shit!

Eigerman jumps from the vehicle, as the retreating posse fire at the Berserkers. It's a useless response. Bloodied but unbowed, the Berserkers run at the vehicles. The woman throws herself out, but Gibbs isn't quick enough. One of the Berserkers pushes the vehicle up the wall of the Necropolis, and Blatz, a small, vicious creature,

stamps on the roof. Inside, Gibbs cowers as the roof is beaten in. He is crushed.

Joyce, who has been watching this entire scene, moves away from the gate towards the Necropolis. The fires are dying down somewhat, and an eerie half-light bathes the scene he moves through. A few surviving posse hurry away, firing at every movement in the shadows.

Back at the gate we see one of the escaping Berserkers flip another car over, while his brothers dispatch posse members. The survivors simply drop their weapons and flee.

237A. SCENE DELETED

237B. SCENE DELETED

238. **INT.**   MAUSOLEUM   NIGHT

The dog-faced man lies dead at the door and beside him Babette, her face subtly bestial. Joyce hears Babette weeping; her cries hit him hard. He goes to her, gathers her up gently in his arms. Babette clings to him; he sees her arms are partially transformed into claws, but he keeps holding her.

Boone emerges from the depths, into the wrecked mausoleum.

BABETTE: Boone . . . [he goes to them] Lori. She's hurt.
BOONE: Where?

Babette points outside.

239. **EXT.**　　　NECROPOLIS　　　NIGHT

Lori runs, Decker follows, his steps steady, relentless and gaining.
Lori takes another stride and the ground gives way beneath her.
She slides down into the earth.

240. **EXT.**　　　NECROPOLIS　　　NIGHT

Boone is tracking them, Joyce following, carrying Babette, who has
a vision.

BABETTE: Falling!

241. **EXT.**　　　BELOW MIDIAN

Chaos, and collapse. Earth is falling all around. Lori picks herself
up and finds her way back up is blocked by debris. She has no
choice but to cross the swaying walkways, while the air thickens
with dust and smoke.
　　There are only one or two Breed left alive down here, desperate-
ly collecting their belongings. They exit the chamber leaving the
smoking bowls . . . We track towards the bowls, as the contents
brighten and bubble.

241A. **INT.**　　　BELOW MIDIAN

Lori descends a flight of stairs, to find Peloquin badly wounded at
the bottom.

PELOQUIN: It's all over. I didn't believe the prophesies and now it's all over.
LORI: What prophesies?

Peloquin takes her arm.

PELOQUIN: You want to see?

241B. **INT.**   ENTRANCE TO MURAL CHAMBER   NIGHT

Peloquin pushes Lori ahead of him.

PELOQUIN: See?

We track towards the mural. Lori can barely believe her eyes. Here, laid out on the walls, is a whole history; and featured amongst its more recent additions, the face of Boone.

PELOQUIN: Yes, it's him.

Boone squatting in front of his fire of love letters. Boone dead in the reeds.

PELOQUIN: All these years waiting for a saviour. But he hasn't saved us. He's destroyed us. I made him, and he's destroyed us.
LORI: Made him?
PELOQUIN: The bite was mine. The bite that mocks death.
LORI: That doesn't make him yours. I belong here on this wall, just as much as you do. Why aren't I here?
PELOQUIN: You're still a Natural. Go back while you've still got a life. Join your tribe.
LORI: That? My tribe? Not any longer.
PELOQUIN: Then die with us. It's over.

Peloquin exits. Lori looks back at the images on the walls once more. Then she exits.

242. **EXT.**   NECROPOLIS   NIGHT

Boone, Joyce and Babette approach the hole where Lori fell.

BABETTE: Let me down. I can't go any further.
BOONE: Why not?
BABETTE [looking down into the hole]: Baphomet.
BOONE [to Joyce]: Take her. Run.

Joyce nods and moves off with her into the smoke. As she disappears, Decker steps forward from the smoke.

DECKER: Quite a dance, huh? Death everywhere and you and me in the middle. Catch!

He throws the head of a Breed at Boone.

    DECKER: Even the dead can die!

Then Decker strikes out at him, slashing at Boone's face. Boone falls backwards. At the last moment he catches hold of Decker, pulling him down into the hole and together they tumble into the earth.

243.   SCENE DELETED

244. **INT.**   MIDIAN

Boone and Decker land on one of the rope bridges. Boone heads across it, pursued by Decker, who slashes at his neck, cutting him.

    DECKER: Almost!

Boone falls back. Decker closes on him, the knives at his neck. The force of his stabs, which miss Boone's neck, break the boards of the bridge. Boone braces his feet beneath Decker and tosses him over. Decker gets up and approaches him again, slashing the ropes of the bridge with his blades as he comes. The fighters connect and struggle, their violent motion carrying them over the edge of the

bridge, dropping them down another level. Decker lands very heavily, and lies still. Boone gets up. His exit along the bridge in one direction is blocked. He has to step past Decker who doesn't move. Only when Boone has stepped beyond him does Decker get up, pursuing Boone across the bridge, and flinging one of the knives at his victim's back. The blade cuts straight through Boone, sticking out from his chest a good six inches. He turns, his fury transforming him into a more extreme creature. Decker comes at Boone with a second blade, slashing at Boone's neck. The battle carries them off the bridge onto the stairs. Decker takes hold of Boone's hair, preparing to deliver the coup de grace. Boone reaches for a weapon, finds a skull, and smashes it into the mask. Decker lets go. Boone tumbles off the stairs, falling face down on a card table.

Decker follows down the stairs. Boone pulls the table off his chest, leaving the Ace of Hearts on the blade in his chest. Decker follows through, driving Boone back into one of the Breed's rooms, where the fight continues. Decker takes a whip from the wall and uses it to disarm Boone, who has snatched up a bone to defend himself with. Boone snatches up a second bone and retaliates, delivering blow after blow against Decker, eventually knocking the knife from his hand and driving him out on to the ledge once more. Decker teeters on the edge, now defenceless. Boone approaches.

BOONE: Want to dance?

He snatches the mask off Decker's face and draws him close, impaling Decker on his own blade. Decker screams.

Then Boone pushes him off the blade, and over the edge of the ledge. Decker falls.

Boone stands on the ledge, and spits down at the corpse. As he does so he hears the same roar from Baphomet that called the Berserkers from harming him. Out of it, comes Baphomet's face.

BAPHOMET [V.O.]: Boone!

244A. **INT.**   LYLESBURG'S CHAMBER

The chamber is empty of life. There are two or three corpses on the floor. We approach the central dais, on which is perched the statue of Baphomet, surrounded by six white heads. Momentarily, lines of light break from the statue's head and strike the white heads, which in turn begin to glow . . .

244B. **INT.**   VARIOUS CHAMBERS

In the chambers we've seen before we see copies of the six statues, in front of which are bowls of Baphomet's fluid . . . They begin to glow, the brightness building. Sparks rise from the fluid.

245. **INT.**   BERSERKERS' CORRIDOR

Lori sits, exhausted, in the corridor. She looks up to see Boone, with the knife still transfixing him.

> LORI: My God . . .
> BOONE: Decker's dead. Take the knife out.

Lori pulls the knife from him, and throws it down.

> BAPHOMET [V.O.]: Boone!
> LORI: Don't go . . .
> BOONE: I'm responsible. I have to.

Lori and Boone head down the corridor, passing Ashberry, who is standing in the shadows.
Lori and Boone head down the stairs towards the chamber.

246. INT.   BAPHOMET'S CHAMBER

Blinding light. As Boone descends into the chamber, he sees eight Nightbreed, surviving members of a Senior Council, Rachel among them, standing around Baphomet. They are wrapping severed limbs of Baphomet, preparing to include him in the exodus. His head and shoulders remain suspended in the light. Baphomet's lips move, making a terrible, eloquent sound. Rachel translates, the deep voice we hear coming from her lips.

RACHEL/BAPHOMET: Come closer . . .

Boone obeys. Baphomet's remaining arm reaches down and holds Boone, as Baphomet's face stares down at him.

RACHEL/BAPHOMET: . . . You have destroyed our refuge . . .
BOONE: I never meant . . .

Baphomet silences him. Boone trembles but maintains eye contact.

RACHEL/BAPHOMET: This was foretold. No refuge is forever. But you are charged . . .
BOONE: Yes . . .
RACHEL/BAPHOMET: . . . You must rebuild what you've destroyed.
BOONE: Where?
RACHEL/BAPHOMET: That you must find yourself. In the world above.
BOONE: I don't . . . I don't know how . . .
RACHEL/BAPHOMET: You shall not be alone. You will find me there and heal me. [holds him close] You are not Boone . . .

And now the words emerge from Baphomet himself, shaking the chamber.

BAPHOMET: . . . you are Cabal!

Boone/Cabal is released. Baphomet is consumed in light. The Council move towards him to finish their task.

LORI [O.S.]: Boone?

Boone/Cabal turns; Lori stands at the bottom of the slope, offering a hand. He takes it, they start up the slope.

Cowering in a niche inside the chamber, out of sight, watching in wonder is Ashberry. Transfixed by Baphomet, he crosses himself.

Boone/Cabal glances back. The Council receive pieces of Baphomet from the light wrapping his smoking fragments in shrouds. The light builds to its brightest level. Pieces of ceiling begin to fall.

246A. **INT.**   VARIOUS CHAMBERS

The bowls start to explode with sparks of white light.

247. **INT.**   BELOW MIDIAN

Boone/Cabal and Lori race up towards the surface, as Midian continues to collapse around them.

248. **INT.**   BAPHOMET'S CHAMBER

Ashberry descends the stairs into the blaze of light. Tears pour
down his cheeks.

He watches as the Council prepare to take down Baphomet's
head.

Near to him is one of the bowls of Baphomet's light. Ashberry
approaches it, hungry for a taste of this glory. He reaches to touch
the bowl. As he does so Baphomet's eyes fix on him. The bowl flips
in the air. The fluid it holds rains down on Ashberry like acid. He
falls back, his body smoking.

249. **EXT.**   NECROPOLIS   NIGHT

Boone/Cabal and Lori reach the surface and race through the ruined
Necropolis, flames all around them. And then, behind them . . .

250. **INT.**   BAPHOMET'S CHAMBER

The tentacles attached to Baphomet's head are detached.

The blaze of light instantly begins to diminish . . .

250A. **INT.**   MIDIAN CORE

The lights start to go out in the core, and earth begins to pour from
the tunnels.

We see it flood the various corridors, with a shuddering roar.

250B. **INT.**   BAPHOMET'S CHAMBER

We glimpse Baphomet's head being covered by the Council, as the
roars increase . . .

251. **EXT.**   OUTSIDE THE GATES   NIGHT

Boone/Cabal and Lori find Joyce, holding Babette, protecting her, near the gates.
    Joyce steps back from the form of Rachel, who pulls her veils around her and holds out her arms.

    RACHEL: Give me my child . . .

Joyce looks at Lori, Boone/Cabal, at Babette and Rachel. He tenderly hands the child over. Rachel holds Babette and they both disappear into the darkness.

    JOYCE [to Boone/Cabal]: . . . I never understood . . . nobody ever told me . . .

He steps away from them and the night engulfs him.

                                        DISSOLVE TO:

252. **INT.**   MIDIAN CORE

The earth has almost obliterated the core entirely.

253. **EXT.**   OUTSIDE THE GATES   NIGHT

The roar ceases. Silence.

254. **EXT.**   NECROPOLIS

Lori and Boone stand in the reeds as the last, bright bloom of the fires dies away on their faces. Figures move away through the smoke, creatures we recognize. The drummer beats out a tattoo as they depart.
    Narcisse appears from the darkness. As he does so, a final explosion roars up from the underground. In the smoke pillar above the site, Baphomet's image momentarily appears before the wind disperses it.

    NARCISSE: Never piss off a God.

Lori looks up into the sky.

                                        CUT TO:

Lori's P.O.V. of the sky, with other Breed, spirits of smoke and light, moving away into the night.

LORI: Where are they going?
NARCISSE: Any hiding place they can find. It'll be dawn soon.
BOONE: When I need you where will I find you?
NARCISSE: You'll find me. And you will need me.

He reaches to shake Boone's hand.

NARCISSE: Never touched a legend before.

He laughs his manic laugh.

NARCISSE [cont.] [to Lori]: Good night, pretty.

He fades into the night, the laughter going with him.

255. **EXT.**   NEAR MIDIAN   NIGHT

In the distance, the burning ruins of Midian. The wind sighs in the moonlit reeds. Cabal and Lori reach the top of the hill, turn and look down, standing apart.

CABAL: I'll have to start tonight.
LORI: I'll go with you, Boone.
CABAL: I'm not Boone, Lori. Do you understand? I belong to the Breed now.
LORI: Then make me belong too; they made you one of them, you can do it to me . . .
CABAL: I can't . . .
LORI: I want to be with you.
CABAL: I'll come back for you when I'm finished . . .
LORI: And when's that gonna be, when I'm ninety and you're still the way you are? I went through hell to find you and you just, just walk away from me? [pause; broken-hearted] Well go on, then, just go. Go on! What more do you want? Leave me some dignity, for Christ's sake!

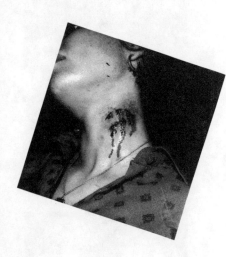

Pause. She turns away, trying not to show him her pain. Cabal turns to go. Lori turns back, sees him going. She can't bear it, looks around, sees Decker's briefcase lying beside the police car. Runs to it, finds a knife.

LORI: Boone!

He turns. She puts the blade to her belly and drives it in.

CABAL: Lori, NO!

She cries out and sinks to the ground in terrible pain. He reaches her and holds her in his arms.

LORI: I lied, I lied, you're all I want.
CABAL: Don't die, God, Lori, don't die . . .
LORI: Well why don't you do something about it, God damn it
. . . remember what you said . . . [fading] . . . quickly . . .

He raises her neck to his mouth. Her eyes flicker closed. He bites. A
fatal, bloody kiss. He rises from her. Her eyes are closed.

CABAL: . . . too late? . . . Oh God, too late . . .

Her eyes open. She's turned.

LORI: You said you'd never leave me.

She grins, presses up to kiss his bloodied mouth. Camera
moves up off them to find the moon and we:

DISSOLVE TO:

255A. **EXT.**   NECROPOLIS   DAY

We track through the ruins of the Necropolis. The walls are black-
ened by fires that are almost extinguished; corpses [human and
Breed] lie in barely distinguishable bundles, from which partially

cremated limbs jut. Smoke hangs in the air. From the distance we see Eigerman, going amongst the corpses, reclaiming guns, bullets and grenades. As we get closer we realize that he is a broken man, his face dirty, his eyes lunatic. He's been crying, the tracks marking the dirt.

Suddenly, he hears a noise, and stands up to see a large figure appearing from the smoke. He goes for his own gun, levelling it at the figure as it approaches.

EIGERMAN: Keep your distance!

The figure keeps coming, emerging from the smoke. It's Ashberry. He has been transformed by the confrontation with Baphomet. His hair has been almost burned away entirely and there is a subtle reconfiguration in the shape of his skull. His clothes are in tatters. There are hints that his once broken body, poisoned by alcohol, has taken on new strength. He looks as insane as Eigerman, but stronger in his lunacy. There's a dangerous fervour in his eyes.

ASHBERRY: I saw their God . . . I saw him . . .
EIGERMAN: What the hell are you talking about?
ASHBERRY: I can still smell him. He's out there . . .

Ashberry walks past Eigerman towards the exit from Necropolis.

EIGERMAN: You mean you can find them?
ASHBERRY: Oh yes.
EIGERMAN: We'll go together then. You can lead me to the bastards. Then I'll wipe them all away.
ASHBERRY: No. They're mine. Their God burned me. I want to burn him back. All of them. Burn them all away.
EIGERMAN: You can't, you don't have the wits . . .

Ashberry turns on him, his face wild. He takes hold of Eigerman by the neck, his fingers digging into the muscle. Blood runs. Eigerman tries to raise the gun but Ashberry takes hold of the man's hand, and summarily snaps his wrist. The gun is dropped. Ashberry starts to lift Eigerman up off the ground. The policeman's flailings stop suddenly. The head lolls. Ashberry flings the body aside, and starts out of the Necropolis. As he approaches the exit he looks up. Sunlight falls on his face.

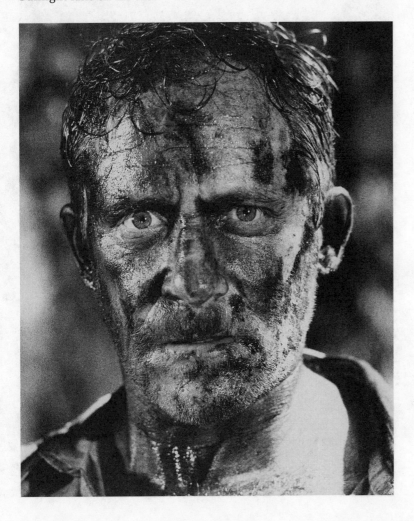

CUT TO:

256. EXT.   MOON   NIGHT

Shining, full. We move down to find a derelict barn, standing alone in a vast field.

DISSOLVE TO:

257. **INT.**   BARN   NIGHT

We track through the darkness to find Rachel, Babette, Kinski and a number of other refugees and children of Midian, staring out at the night.

BABETTE: . . . who will come for us?
KINSKI: His name is Cabal. He unmade Midian.
BABETTE: How soon?
RACHEL: On the next wind. If not tonight, then tomorrow.

Babette gazes out over the cornfields.

BABETTE: On the next wind . . .

DISSOLVE TO:

258. **EXT.**   HILL   NIGHT

Cabal and Lori, standing on the hill, against a background of stars.

BABETTE [V.O.]: . . . if not tonight . . . tomorrow . . .

DISSOLVE TO:

259. **INT.**   BELOW MIDIAN   NIGHT

Moving through the ruined chambers, illuminated by dying flickers of flame, we find and track along the end of the heroic mosaic/mural. It tells, in a rush of images, the story of the ruin of Midian.
   Camera comes to a stop on the final image: Cabal and Lori, as we just saw them, on a hill, framed against the star-filled heavens.
   The sound of the wind . . .
   Fade to black.

JAMES G. ROBINSON AND JOE ROTH

PRESENT

A MORGAN CREEK PRODUCTION OF

CLIVE BARKER'S
NIGHTBREED

CRAIG SHEFFER   ANNE BOBBY
DAVID CRONENBERG   CHARLES HAID

MUSIC BY
DANNY ELFMAN

SPECIAL MAKE-UP AND VISUAL EFFECTS
IMAGE ANIMATION

SOUND DESIGN BY
BRUCE NYZNIK

EDITED BY
RICHARD MARDEN AND
MARK GOLDBLATT

PRODUCTION DESIGNER
STEVE HARDIE

DIRECTOR OF PHOTOGRAPHY
ROBIN VIDGEON BSC

EXECUTIVE PRODUCERS
JAMES G. ROBINSON AND JOE ROTH

BASED ON CLIVE BARKER'S
CABAL

PRODUCED BY
GABRIELLA MARTINELLI

WRITTEN AND DIRECTED BY
CLIVE BARKER